## GO UP FOR GLORY

"This, then, is my story. It begins in what seems the long ago. . . . I do not know where it will end, but like any man I have my hopes and dreams and goals. Goals, which for me far transcend mere basketball. I said once that basketball was basically a child's game and certainly nothing which can ever be compared with the contributions of a Salk or a Stevenson. It has been a great game for me and I have loved it, but it is one more stop-over in the course which I must follow, a course which I hope will one day permit me to contribute more to America and more to the Negroes of America."

# Go Up for Glory

# BILL RUSSELL

## as told to
### William McSweeny

A BERKLEY MEDALLION BOOK
PUBLISHED BY COWARD, McCANN & GEOGHEGAN, INC.
DISTRIBUTED BY BERKLEY PUBLISHING CORPORATION

To our children . . . in the hope that they will grow up
as we could not . . . equal . . . and understanding.
William  Felton  Russell
William  Francis  McSweeny

---

Not what we give, but what we share . . .
for the gift without the giver is bare.
—James  Russell  Lowell

---

COPYRIGHT © 1966 BY WILLIAM FELTON
RUSSELL and WILLIAM FRANCIS McSWEENY

SBN 425-2162-9

*Coward, McCann & Geoghegan, Inc.*
*200 Madison Avenue*
*New York, N.Y. 10016*

*Berkley Publishing Corporation*
*200 Madison Avenue*
*New York, N.Y. 10016*

BERKLEY MEDALLION BOOKS ® TM 757,375

Printed in the United States of America

COWARD, McCANN & GEOGHEGAN, INC.–BERKLEY
MEDALLION EDITION, DECEMBER, 1966
2nd Printing, April, 1967
3rd Printing, June, 1969
4th Printing, October, 1969
5th Printing, October, 1970
6th Printing, September, 1971
7th Printing, January, 1972
New Edition, March, 1972 (8th Printing)

## Contents

# FOREWORD

There are no alibis in this book.

There are no untruths.

There is, within these pages, only a view of the world as I see it. It is based on my opinions . . . but not on prejudice.

One year ago, I would not have considered even the possibility of writing such a book. I felt I had not lived enough or done enough. One year from now, I may regret that I did not extend further passages. Ten years hence, I may have altered my philosophy or, at least, some of my opinions.

The one certainty is that a man can never be certain of what he thinks. He can only strive and learn and fight against the frustrations of his life and continue that struggle to the point that he develops a philosophy.

A man who must ask for a philosophy will never have one. My philosophy is only the result of what has happened in this life.

I can honestly say that I have never worked to be liked. J have worked only to be respected. If I am liked, then that is an extra, valued bonus of the world we inhabit. If I am disliked, it is the privilege of those who wish to dislike me—as long as it is not based on prejudice.

What has my life been?

Many things. Many places. Many conquests. Many failures.

We live at a time of the greatest changes in the history of mankind. It has been a fierce time and a time of fierce loves and hates and issues.

I have fought in every way I know how. I fought because I believed it was right to fight. I think that no man should fear the consequences because every man must do that which he believes is right.

I have worked for money and I have made large sums of it. But I never worshiped money. I have worshiped little and fought only for the rights of man, all men, all races, all religions.

In the course of writing this book, I found myself asking once again:

"Who am I?

"What am I?

"Where am I going?"

Perhaps I will always march to the distant drum. Perhaps I will never catch the beat of the tune. But I will try.

On these pages, I try. Here, in the thirty-first year of my life, is the story of the way my life has been.

It is a story which can be read on three levels.

The story of an American.

The story of a Negro.

The story of a professional basketball player.

At each level, I can only say that these are straightforward truths. Regardless of how it goes, there will never be any alibis.

WILLIAM FELTON RUSSELL

# CHAPTER I

## THE KID

Before me lay seven feet of black death, circling.

Each time it moved, the circle grew smaller and came closer to me.

I raised the gun and I fired, pumping rapidly, firing three shots.

The black death raised its head at me and sneered and slithered away into the jungle, down into the dark morass and oblivion of the wetness.

I dropped the shotgun and stood there transfixed and the African sun beat down through the rubber trees and the snake—the Black Mamba, the Black Death—was gone.

But my whole life had run before my eyes in those seconds. It is true. It happens. Flashes of what was and what might have been and what shouldn't have been. My victories. My mistakes. My glories. My disenchantments.

Who am I? What am I? Where am I going? That is what I thought standing there in the sunlight with the smell of the powder and the gun lying at my feet.

I had asked the question silently long before. Perhaps I had been asking the question all of my life. But the Black Death brought it pouring from my lips, emptying into the orderly rows of the rubber trees and the disorder and death of the jungle bushes.

This, then, is my story. It begins in what seems the long ago, certainly a far, far distance from the rubber plantation which I began in Liberia after the world championships of 1960. I do not know where it will end, but like any man I have my hopes and dreams and goals. Goals, which for me far transcend mere basketball. I said

9

once that basketball was basically a child's game and certainly nothing which can ever be compared with the contributions of a Salk or a Stevenson. It has been a great game for me and I have loved it, but it is one more stopover in the course which I must follow, a course which I hope will one day permit me to contribute more to America and more to the Negroes of America.

It is a life that has been lived strongly, even when it has been misdirected and wasted in anger. As you read it, know only that I wrote this book not to preach, nor to beg, nor in the bigotry which can be as much the fault of the Negro as the white man. It is just the story of a boy who became the man standing in the sunshine with the Black Death looking at him, and fired the gun and wondered who he was.

I am, I guess, just a man. No better. No worse.

So do a slow dissolve, baby, as they say in the movies, into black.

And the black begins . . . with Russell in Monroe, Louisiana.

In the prewar period of the thirties and early forties, growing up in the Deep South did not have as disturbing an effect on me as visiting it in 1944, or 1956, or 1962. When you're a kid, you just never realize that there is a tremendous basic difference between mere existence and freedom.

At least, I didn't.

I was just a kid who liked his friends and loved his mother and father and brother and scuffed along the dirt road, laughing, on my way to a barn that was converted into a school.

Still, there was something deep and underlying—a disquieting factor—the exact nature of which I am probably still not fully aware. I remember I was fascinated with the trains that went by and spent many afternoons at the fence watching and waving at the engineers. Twenty years later, I spent a good portion of my first salary on an extensive layout of electric trains. Perhaps to satisfy a promise I never knew I made. Perhaps to reach a goal I never knew I set. Perhaps. The trains have been played with by many friends since. Then, finally, I put them away. I wonder if perhaps it wasn't closing a chapter in my life.

My father, Charles Russell, had a job in a paper bag factory. It was what we in the Black South called "a Negro job." There was advancement, but it was limited.

Charlie Russell was not a man who was ever going to be kept back, however, and because he was a man, he broke the bonds eventually and left, moving first to Detroit and finally to California.

There were things a man simply could not tolerate in Louisiana.

Flashing memories come back, memories more bitter now than the events themselves, because at the moment of occurrence these insults seemed to be absolute facts of existence, which couldn't be overcome. It was a little like being afloat and slowly drowning in a vast sea of tar.

Once we went to the ice house and the attendant just let us sit in the car for fifteen or twenty minutes while he talked to another white man. That man drove off and another car came along and the attendant went to wait on those people, so my father began driving off.

The attendant ran over to my Dad's window and said:

"Don't you ever try to do that, boy. Unless you want to get shot."

He had a big gun.

My dad picked up a tire iron and got out of the car and the red-neck just turned and ran for his life and my heart overflowed with wonder and pride for my father. It does to this moment when I look back to what he was facing.

But, Louisiana wasn't the place for him.

There were other things you just couldn't cope with because you couldn't stand up to them, face to face.

My mother, Katie, was a gentle woman. In that time, women affected modified riding habits as stylish street clothes. Katie was awfully proud of her suit, but one day she was shopping in Monroe and a cop came up to her and said:

"Who do you think you are, nigger? Dressing like a

11

white woman. Get out of town before sundown or I'll throw you in jail."

My mother came home in a state of shock.

The memory lingers on of the five-year-old boy who watched that woman sitting in the kitchen of her home, trying to understand, trying to comprehend this unwarranted viciousness.

Faced with this—and being a man and the head of the house—my father struck out for freedom. He went to Oakland, California. We remained behind in Monroe until our father was able to send for us.

It was not all insult and injury by any means. My brother Charlie and I had our laughs as well as our tears.

To this day, I still chuckle at one gag we pulled. A peglegged man with an enormously fat wife was a regular visitor to our home. Fascinated with ghosts, they would spend hours discussing the more recent "appearances" of strange images in the district.

One particular evening, they talked on and on, late into the night. Charlie and I pulled off our bed-sheets, finally, and went down the road to wait. Eventually the little pegleg man and the fat wife ended their visit. When they came along past our bush, we jumped out, going "who-who-whooo."

Did you ever see a man with a pegleg race a fat wife?

But being a Negro in Louisiana can have its drawbacks.

My brother and I went down to look at a golf course. We weren't planning to play. We knew better.

We had never seen one, so we just went to look over the fence.

Now, we were walking home and throwing stones at each other—not maliciously, just pebbles that we were skipping back and forth—and a guy came by in his car and a pebble hit it.

He chased us all over the backroads. We couldn't get away from him. He finally caught me on the edge of a field. I was seven years old and winded, but I was ready to start running again. He got out of the car and started for me and he said:

"I catch you, nigger, I'm gonna hang you."

The gentleman did not get any closer.

I ran off, half angry, half laughing. Much later in life, I can laugh more. Probably just some poor bum who had a bad day on the golf course.

When my dad was settled in Oakland we received the word—and the money—to come and join him.

The image of the Negro who always eats chicken and carries his lunch on public transportation is part of American folklore.

I can explain it best by pointing out that all trains in the south were segregated. Negroes couldn't eat in the diner and the only food which would last on a long trip was chicken. So we took our chicken and rode in our segregated car from Louisiana to Little Rock to St. Louis before the rules changed and we could ride in any compartment of the streamliner which took us on to California.

Freedom, a new form of freedom, lay ahead.

Behind was a world which I will continue to fight to my dying breath. Ahead was a world which also had to be fought. And understood. And, in a fashion, conquered.

We moved into the north section of Oakland, sometimes known unaffectionately as "Landlord's Paradise."

It was a regular house with a regular garage, except that eight families were living in the eight rooms and one family was living in the garage. Pigs and sheep and chickens were raised in the backyard. A rotten, filthy hole. A firetrap with light bulbs hanging off uncoated wires.

It was the only place we could find. It was, the landlord said, the war.

War brings out the humanitarians among us.

But Oakland, compared with Louisiana, was Paradise gained.

We finally moved into the project by Cole School. It was an integrated project, integrated to the extent that the whites lived in one section and the Negroes lived in another. We were reasonably happy. We had achieved stature, even by moving into a project, and we remained there until I joined the Celtics.

It was in the project yard that I first learned to play

13

basketball. We "organized" a backboard and a ball. Some people "liberate." Our group "organized."

And we lived. My mother and father were both working in the shipyards and one worked days and one nights, so there was always someone home. It was 1943, a good year, and a happy one.

Beneath it lurked a latent feeling, an instinct which every Negro develops. Talk now of the riot in Watts, Los Angeles, in 1965, but if you want to understand what might have happened in Watts, or anywhere else, understand certain factors which every Negro in this period learned.

It was as much a lesson as any which was taught to us in the fourth grade at the Cole School.

It stood out, harsh and unyielding, a wall which understanding still cannot penetrate.

You are a Negro. You are less.

It covered every area. A living, smarting, hurting, smelling, greasy substance which covered you. A morass to fight from.

The Oakland Police at this time were mostly southerners. They worked from a double standard. There are memories which still sear. A Fourth of July celebration at the Park. The kids went up. We were ten-, eleven-, twelve-year-olds. There was an argument between gangs. Not a scheduled riot. A beef between four or five boys. The cops arrested one kid and beat and kicked him as they dragged him off. He was eleven years old.

My brother Charlie wanted to earn some extra money. He was twelve years old. He built a shoe shine box. He bought some polish. He went out to shine shoes. The police arrested him for shining shoes. There were white boys doing it, but they were just told to move on. They arrested my brother Charlie because he was a little black boy and they took him to the station and booked him and for all the rest of his life my brother would have a police record.

For shining shoes?

When you are twelve years old?

You are little, but you learn fast. Be off the street by five o'clock. Move fast if you are little and black. Keep moving. Because the police will get you and book

14

you and maybe kick you. Because you are black. And a child wonders: Why did they do it? What does it make me? Am I nothing? Am I a non-person?

The Oakland Police brought in several Negro policemen. But they did not stop any problems. Everyone knew they were policemen who could not arrest white people. The double standard was in force.

What happens?

Reflectively, from the depths of the lessons learned —and, I hope, from the heights of a world partially conquered—these facts come forward:

The police represent society. White society. The Negro learns to hate authority. And the Negro also learns to hate himself. They are taught through repetition that they are the scum of the earth and they are bad. They have nothing in common with anyone, not even with each other. They are at the bottom of the heap, the bottom of the dung heap.

They become more and more frustrated. They lose respect for themselves and they lose respect for society. Pretty soon you develop a hatred for yourself. And then you lose all association. That is what happened to the Negro in this time, in this place. That is why there has been a Harlem riot and a Detroit riot and a Watts riot.

The burden was placed upon them by the power structure, which broke down their society to the point that there was no identification, no pride.

For me, it was different. Oakland then was still better than Monroe, Louisiana. And I began reading. I read Richard Halliburton's *Seven Wonders of the World.*

He wrote of the Citadel in Haiti and of Henri Christophe. History has judged Henri Christophe harshly. He was mad. He was a despot. Yet, in my young mind, this was the first identification with a Negro who was a leader. Years later, I went to Haiti just to see the Citadel. I saw the deprived of Haiti, the deprivations of the government, the fear of the people. My wife and I were even arrested for being out at night in the back country. I saw fear, felt fear, tasted fear of a different kind, a fear imposed on Negroes by Negroes.

Yet, to this very day, I cannot in my mind fix upon Henri Christophe as a bad man. For he was the first hero of my youth. A black man who became the dominant force in a power structure.

Right? Wrong? I do not know. But there are young Negro boys in America this day, this night, who read. And dream.

Later, much later, one night when I was sixteen, I went to bed just a boy. I woke up the next morning proud—so very proud—to be a Negro. The pride has ever since been with me. I could not put my finger on what triggered this emotion. But it was there. I remember it still. So vividly. Walking and going to the kitchen for breakfast with a pride which has never left me. Perhaps, in turn, it gave me the impetus to fight the power structure and to go forward.

It happened. Just that way.

Other things happened as well. One day I came home from school and my mother was not there. She was in the hospital and she was sick.

Two weeks later she was dead.

I never found out why. She was thirty-two and she was dead. My father came home and he woke up Charlie and me and he sat on the bed and said: "We'll all have to stick together now." I remember I had a warm, cozy feeling. We were all together.

We took her home to Louisiana, home to lie beside her people, in her earth.

While we were there, we went to visit an old friend of my father's.

He was rich. My father was poor. He was white. My father was black.

But they were men together and they fished together and laughed together and of all the men who had come and gone in our lives, Charlie and I always remembered him as my father's friend, as the man of whom my father and mother always spoke warmly.

We went to visit him and they talked while my brother and I sat there and then he said:

"Yeah, Charlie. You always were a good nigger."

It comes back to me even now. The cold whiplash of an anger, of a frustration.

He was my father's friend.

They fished together. They laughed together. They were men together.

But "Charlie was always a good nigger."

In front of his children. Powerless to do anything. Powerless to answer here in the Deep South—the Black South—of Louisiana.

We left our "friend" and went home.

My father had developed a trucking business with farmers in the San Joaquin Valley. It was a good business, paying good money. He had to give up the business. He had two sons to raise. He went to work in a foundry at $40 a week. I look back on it now and I feel a kinship with my father. I did not understand at the time and I did not like many things he did.

But he was always a man. He was young and strong and the world was before him and he could have left us in Louisiana with our aunts. Instead, he brought us back to California and, as best he could, he raised us.

There was separation. There was loneliness. From the day my mother died, my father never again saw our report cards. Charlie signed mine. I signed Charlie's. Yet I appreciate what he tried to do.

Now, in this time, I would never make a judgment on him. He is, simply, my father.

In 1965 when I signed my contract as a $100,001-a-year basketball player I called him and said I didn't want him ever to work again.

He provided me with one of the great laughing moments of my life.

"Of course I'm going to work," he said. "I've given that place eighteen good years out of my life. Now, I'll give them a couple of bad years."

For me, the bad years were both beginning and ending, for I was moving on towards High School—and to basketball. It was a strange, long course, but it brought me to where I am today.

Charlie—two years ahead of me—was a good athlete and transferred from junior high to Oakland Tech, which was something of a status symbol in our neighborhood. It was the case of a Negro managing to break the bonds, break the barrier and fight from under the pile heaped on

17

him. Oakland Tech was predominantly white, while Mc-Clymonds was ninety-five percent Negro.

Charlie went on to become a really standout athlete. I remained behind to begin a period of sliding backwards. I didn't realize it at the time, but Charlie had a very strong effect on me. I admired him tremendously and he was a figurehead of sorts. Perhaps because I didn't know him, I felt that he was always in command of the situation while I, on the other hand, was always flummoxing things up.

Almost as a competitive thing which society creates, I was forced into basketball, forced into it, number one as "Charlie's kid brother" and, secondly, because I wanted to follow in his footsteps.

Alas, "Charlie's kid brother" couldn't even make the home room basketball team.

Charlie took an awful fall in pride one day with my dad. Charlie could run the 100 in 10:4 and he was bragging about it. "C'mon," my father said, "I'll race you."

My father had just finished working all day. He had on those heavy factory shoes, but they went out on the sidewalk in front of the project and we paced off a hundred yards. They ran it—a dead heat.

I don't know how it affected my brother, but it left me with a great feeling of pride in my dad, one that still exists, although our relationship has always been a passionate one, blowing hot and cold as whims and wills have controlled it.

I very nearly failed the eighth grade. This experience was so shocking to me, so humiliating that it spurred me on to buckle down and begin studying. I became a fairly good student after that.

Unable to make a sports team, and further handicapped by being a split-year student (we began our ninth grade in January, for example), I went out for the band. My uncle had bought a clarinet for me. I didn't last long. For one thing, I couldn't play the darn thing and keep time with my foot simultaneously. I was always off key.

More important, the Hoover Junior High music teacher fancied using a paddle to smack kids. He thought that would include Russell, but Russell didn't buy that and we parted company rapidly.

Then I transferred into the tenth grade at McClymonds High. From there things didn't go so well, either. The only good luck I had—and a great piece of luck it was—came when a white teacher named George Powles, who had been my homeroom instructor at Hoover, transferred over as well.

Powles, Miss Helen Bunton and Mr. Earl Swisher were three unusual teachers at this school. They had true empathy with the human race, which they demonstrated by their deep consideration for the students. The teachers who wanted to help the Negro students improve themselves were not held in high regard by the administration. It cost some of them dearly.

After I finished at the University of San Francisco, Mr. Swisher told me that when I entered the college some of the McClymonds teachers got up a pool on how long I would last.

The negative influence of the average teacher cannot be stressed strongly enough. I had a counselor at high school, a lady who wanted to put me in a straight shop course. She wouldn't even hear of my going to college.

Another favorite device used to discourage students was to put them in a program called "job training."

It was divided between IWE—inside work experience —and EWE. I never figured out what EWE was. In IWE though, you took a period a week in which you just ran errands for the teacher. EWE, you did exercises with the gym teacher. This is preparing a boy to compete in life? This is study?

The teachers carried tremendous weight. They had so much influence that they could even guide girls and boys into who was going to date whom and I sincerely believe a lot of unhappy, early marriages were created, later dissolved, all because these teachers were so misguided in their educational philosophy.

There was a boy who wanted to go to the U. of California. His teacher told him flat out in front of the class, "You're not smart enough," and flunked him in English. He was a fighter. He went to the school board and they reversed the decision and he went on to the U. of Cal. where he graduated *cum laude*.

But you didn't get there without a fight.

Most certainly, all of this was a misguided theory which has caused much of the trouble exploding all around us in the Sixties.

Teach the boy a trade. Teach him to do something menial, because that's the only kind of job he'll get anyway.

Powles . . . Miss Bunton . . . Mr. Swisher were of a different breed.

Powles certainly wasn't going to give me any breaks, but he still was a man guided by deep, instinctual feelings of our common humanity.

There was another coach named Mangini. Football. I went out for it, trying to make defensive end on the Mc-Clymonds Warriors. Mangini ran the first ten plays around my end in a scrimmage one day.

It was an impersonal thing for him perhaps, but it nearly broke my spirit. I quit. Mangini was not all wrong, but I could never like him now, and to any high school coach I must add this one thought: When it seems like nothing to you, don't count on the fact that it is nothing for the boy. It might be very important.

I finally wound up hoping to be a cheerleader and, failing that (I wasn't doing so good in these days, as you can see), I became more or less just the official mascot.

Next I tried my hand at basketball. Powles was the Jay-Vee coach. A man named Fitzpatrick coached the varsity. I went out for it, but I didn't make it. Fitzpatrick had a fabulous rep as a coach and a rep for being tough. Just at this time my brother Charlie was going great guns for Oakland Tech and the day I was cut, Fitzpatrick said in front of the squad: "Why is it that if there are two brothers in school we always get the bum?"

It left me shaken.

Nearly broken.

In 1958, ten years later, the Celtics were playing an exhibition in Hawaii and the phone rang in my room and there was good old Fitzpatrick on the other end. He

20

wanted me to come to dinner with some friends so they could meet one of McClymonds' "old boys."

I was courteous. I was tempted. I just said I had made prior plans.

He probably never even knew what he did to me. It wasn't a vendetta. Just a stray thing to him. To me, it was a crushing blow.

I wonder how many other kids in this world may have been injured the same way.

What with all these developments going against me, I was ready to pack it in. I remember I was going by the gym one day and Art Ison, who was the janitor, said: "I haven't seen you around lately."

"These guys are just better than me. I couldn't make it," I answered.

He hit me with a telling bit of philosophy: "If you think so, Russell, then they always will be."

Just at that point, Powles stuck his two cents in. He told me to come out for the JayVees. I dragged my feet, but I came out. I didn't break any records. I was terrible. But Powles had faith in me as a person and didn't want to break my spirit.

He only had fifteen uniforms for the team, but he carried sixteen players. I was the sixteenth and I split the uniform with a boy named Roland Campbell.

By that one gesture, I believe that man saved me from becoming a juvenile delinquent. If I hadn't had basketball, all of my energies and frustrations would surely have been carried in some other direction.

I went to the games and practiced although I didn't play much. Powles gave me $2 to join the Boys Club and I played every afternoon and night in the pickup scrimmages. I was so skinny that I had to keep moving in the shower to get wet.

In my senior year, thanks to him, I was starting to understand something about the game. Remember, I was a "splitter." I went from January to January, so my senior year actually covered half of each season.

I was 6-5 now and I weighed 160 and I was anything but a killer. I couldn't get angry at anybody. Bobby Woods, who now plays for the Harlem Magicians, was my buddy, supposedly, but I couldn't understand him sometimes because he would get on my back and really hack me. I didn't know that Powles was making him do it to stir me up. It worked. If I hadn't been a coward I would have whacked that Woods in the mouth.

There have been stories around that I could have been a real good heavyweight fighter. Forget it, baby, I admit it. I was the fastest kid in Oakland—with my feet. Fist fighting I only did when there was no way around it and I was always looking to get around.

There was another thing about fighting. Before we started, Powles—the white coach—called us in. "You might as well face it," he said. "You are a Negro team and the second there's any trouble everyone is going to blame you, whether it's your fault or not. You'll be guilty. The slightest trouble and everybody will claim it was a riot. Remember that. We've got an extra burden here. But we can carry it. We'll play with it and win, right?"

Oakland offers the Keyes Memorial Trophy to the team and student body that demonstrates the best sportsmanship. We won it three years in a row. I was proud of that. I am proud of it, still. It's a big thing, a big tribute to those players and those students—and that man.

In our senior year, we just seemed to run away and hide from the other schoolboys. It just came to us, all at once. Powles put it there over those years, but now everything fell into place.

We came up to my January graduation and were matched in the biggest game I had every played—Oakland High. I was paired against All City All Star Truman Bruce.

I scored my career high—fourteen points—and we beat them badly. I hadn't realized it, but Hal DeJulio was watching the game. DeJulio was an ex-University of San Francisco player. He was casually scouting on his own and considering Bruce for a USF scholarship. After watching the game, he picked me.

I was dumbfounded, ecstatic. High school was over for me with that game. As a split-session student, I was graduating. McClymonds went on to win the city championship and I went off on a trip through British Co-

22

lumbia and the northwest with a schoolboy All Star team. I went with a college scholarship in my pocket. Next September, I would be in college, not in a foundry.

It wasn't much. Board, room, tuition and books for the first year and no spending money for the first year, in return for which I was required to wait table and wash dishes.

But to me, it was the most beautiful . . . greatest . . . thing in the world. On that trip my entire game suddenly developed. Perhaps it was the security of knowing I was going to college.

I felt a little less secure when so many people didn't even know there was a University of San Francisco.

And even more insecure when I travelled across the Bay three times and couldn't find the school. No one knew where it was. But I finally found it.

It was a lucky find.

# CHAPTER II

# NATIONAL CHAMPIONS

A small school that I couldn't find.

A tall guy no one else wanted.

It was a strange combination. To me, it was a thing of rare beauty. They didn't even have a gym. But it was college . . . college!

Much later, after we began winning, many colleges came around with offers which were considerably more than washing dishes and gassing cars. I laughed them away. USF and I were together. I was with them as long as they were with me.

As the years have gone by, the college scholarship for athletics has come under attack. Are they good or bad? Answer: yes and no.

Mine certainly wasn't about to make a cheating, lying thief out of me. That was certain.

It was a room, an education and a job which paid no money during the first season. I'd take it again if I had to.

My roommate was a handsome kid named K.C. Jones. K.C., that's all. Just the initials. You know the story *The Quiet Man?* That could be the title of K.C.'s life.

He was a sophomore when I moved in with him. He was also affluent. As a sophomore, he was receiving board, tuition, and—unbelievable wealth—$30 a month. A millionaire.

For one whole month he didn't talk to me. Nothing. Not a word. Not hello. Not goodbye. Not a single word.

I had the top bunk. He had the bottom. He also had the alarm clock. For thirty straight days the routine went like this. The alarm rings. K.C. gets dressed. Russell hunkers under the covers. K.C. starts out the door and slams the side of the bunk:

"RUSSELL."

Russell jumps out onto the floor and starts rushing down to get something to eat before the bell rings. K.C. sits opposite me. Never a word. Chomp. Chomp. The square eyes.

I began talking to myself in the room. Something had to be wrong with me. Then I walked in one day and K.C. just started talking. Nothing was wrong. K.C. was just shy. He always has been. He is a brilliant man who, at this writing, is about to join the faculty at Brandeis University. He has travelled the world and has had some fantastic experiences and is perhaps the best-loved player in professional sports, both by outsiders and by participants. And if you know him really well, he will say perhaps four words in the course of the day.

Just plain shy.

On the Celtics we call him: "The Man With the Square Eyes." He just sits there all day long on the road trips watching the TV screen.

Maybe he made a mistake talking to me. Here I was suddenly hobnobbing with an aristocrat among athletes, a fat cat getting a whole $30 a month.

From that moment on, everywhere that K.C. went, Russell was sure to follow. He wanted an ice cream cone? He bought two. He wanted to go to the movies? He bought two tickets. It was K.C. and me and $30 a month.

What kind of a man was he, even then? This kind. I needed a pair of shoes. Holes in each sole. K.C. and I were walking along and he took me into a shoe store and bought me a pair. No words. Just plain bought me the pair of shoes.

He never has to say a word to me. That kind of friendship isn't purchased—with words or money.

Actually, my economic distress was the result of my own pigheadedness. An argument with my father. K.C. didn't know my dad at that time, but he suffered accordingly.

The argument with my dad had come in September, just before I went to school. I worked the summer in the shipyard. The Admiral was like so many of them.

25

He was out to set a record for U.S. saving bond purchases. Everyone in the yard had to buy a bond. Then you took them across the street and peddled them to a broker and got your money back—or most of it.

I saved up $150 in bonds and during the summer I told my dad to hold it for me. You know, make the old man feel close to you.

In September, I wanted the bonds to buy some clothes. He wouldn't give them to me. He wanted me to save them for a rainy day. For me, it was pouring.

We argued.

We didn't speak again until February. He came to every game, but I didn't speak and neither did he.

We were both ridiculous. Meantime, K.C. was trying to stuff the hole in my financial dike. I'm a big guy. It was a large hole.

And I was trying to learn to stuff the ball in the hole. There was distress here as well.

Phil Woolpert, the USF coach, had an entirely different idea about the way Russell would play basketball. Woolpert and I had our misunderstandings, more of a personal thing than an element which interfered with our basketball. He was an excellent technician, but he did not fully understand men.

Woolpert wanted me to play in the same fashion as his former center, who had been 6-5. I was 6-10. My style was defense, plus shooting. We established a détente of sorts. I was to be a scorer, but in my own mind I was concentrating on learning everything I could about defense—and about blocking shots.

USF was entering a new phase in its history. A small Jesuit college, it had no gym, and the basketball players would become known as the "Homeless Dons" as we gained attention with two national championships. Ultimately, the profits from our attraction at the various gates were to build USF a very large gym indeed.

It is one of the unique characteristics of American education that a gym and a football field are as important as a science laboratory. Schools seek national reputations and money through sports in order to add to the scholastic capabilities of the college and to increase enrollment. At the same time they must keep the alumni happy by making them proud of the old school's ability to win the pennants.

It would seem in the cold, crass world of business that a man would be prouder of a college that provided a good education than one noted for the muscularity of its athletes, but such will never be the case.

In misguided combine, the alumni, educators and coaches have created a climate of confusion and chaos which vastly weakens the moral fiber of our young men. Scholarship programs no longer are concerned with education. Scholarships are only a financial device which places so much pressure on the athlete that he begins cheating. The player is taught it is not just how you play the game that counts. If you want to get paid, baby, you better play to win—and at the same time get passing marks.

So athletes are caught cheating and the educators, coaches and alumni suddenly go around with a long face saying: "That ingrate. He cheated us."

Where did he learn to cheat?

Paul Hornung recently delivered himself of a book on what might be considered an interesting career. I believe he is symptomatic of our times. On the one hand his athletic abilities cast him into a fairy-tale world where the rules were different. On the other, he approaches—as the years progress—that more mundane, real world, where the fairy-tale does not apply.

Hornung was caught betting on football. His apologies were profound. He went home to his mother. He vowed reform and was even lionized by some sportswriters, parents and educators to the extent that many youngsters wrote messages of sympathy and understanding.

Pardon my snort. What can possibly be happening in the United States when an athlete, who writes as much about kiss-and-tell as he does about football, and who keeps two different sets of scorecards, becomes a national hero when he is caught betting?

Don't just blame Hornung. He's only an example. He learned the rules somewhere.

It is extremely difficult to be an All-American and still maintain a high scholastic average. You have to live the sport. You have to practice and travel, day and night,

27

and you find it pretty difficult to study after three or four hours of practice.

This is not an excuse for athletes, but a fact. Statements are often made which infer that athletes, by and large, are stupid. Not so. Not any more than anyone else. Some are stupid. Some aren't. But they can't carry both loads—academic and sports.

The colleges don't make it any easier. They want a winner. The coach wants a winner to keep his job. The alumni want a winner. The athlete's scholarship only increases as he wins and many a kid who breaks a leg and can't play anymore finds that his scholarship terminates at the end of the school year.

The alumni put the pressures on. On both the coach and the player. Win, baby, and you're driving a big convertible, courtesy of good old Mr. Jones, Class of '24. Win, baby, and buy yourself $500 worth of clothes, charge it to Mr. Smith, Class of '31. Win, baby, and come on over to my house and meet the folks. Be the big hero of the party. Don't worry about studies. If it gets too burdensome then there's always a prof who'll help bail you out.

But lose. Oh my, don't lose. Because if you lose then the coach is under pressure. Then the financial gate falls off for the school. The only way to solve a problem such as this is to recognize it. It is basic nature for man to be a lazy animal. Give a man a break and first he accepts it and next begins expecting it. This is what has happened tô college athletics.

Cheating has become more and more prevalent. Tragically, it is more often than not excused, and therefore condoned. There is no excuse. Anyway you cut it, cheating is cheating—robbery of the spirit.

I have seen athletes spend more hours figuring ways to cheat than were required to pass the examinations fairly.

I did not cheat. I considered it. I had to draw the line somewhere. I was not USF's most brilliant student and if I had cheated I most probably would have graduated in 1956. It has not been previously told, but I did not graduate from the University of San Francisco. I was twice the star of a national champion. I went from college to the Olympics. But I could not compete and carry all the required courses, so I decided on the sport and planned to make up the courses later. I was sixteen units shy of graduation—the equivalent of one semester.

But to go back to the basic premise, the whole climate can be corrected if the educators, the coaches and the alumni face it squarely. Make it mandatory that a boy-man—because this is what the average college athlete still is, a boy-man—attends college for an education. If grades or sport must suffer, then make it the sport. Play fair with the kid. One possible solution would be to make the scholarship good for as long as it takes the student to graduate. Regardless of how long he plays ball.

Another: If any athlete doesn't have it, then flunk him out. Don't carry him on soft courses just to keep him eligible.

A third: If you want just a professional athlete student, then stop fooling around and just plain hire professionals.

The days are gone when a student was a big man on the campus and easily recognizable and identified with the school. You take a campus of 25,000 now. Who knows the guy who plays on the football team? So, just hire pros and forget it.

Stop hiding behind the guise of intellectual amateurism and do something decent for these kids. Like sending them forth into the world equipped to deal with it, not just as poor, mixed-up, sometimes fat-headed athletes.

Unless this is done, or some similar action taken, there will be more and more scandals and our young people will feel more and more sorry for the big star who gets caught.

And there will be more and more who will get caught.

At USF we were fortunate. We didn't have them. Perhaps because we were such a small school. We had our hands full with other problems.

Such as trying to win that national championship. We were starting off at a school that was a nothing. No one knew much about us. They still didn't know about us in

29

my freshman year of 1952, except around the Bay Area.

They might have found out in 1953. We were ready for the big leagues. Woolpert had found some players. I was 6-10 now and I had developed a hook shot and a stuff shot and the blocked shot.

We opened against the University of California, which was heavily favored. They had a great center in Bob McKeen. He tried hard, but we ate him up. K.C. had been sick going to the game, but he played, and with K.C. backing me, I blocked thirteen shots, held McKeen to fourteen points and scored twenty-three.

The key to it was K.C., but K.C. was playing the game with appendicitis. The quiet man, the stoic. He never complained. When the doctor asked him if it hurt he said: "A little."

By that time he was halfway to the hospital with a ruptured appendix and we were halfway down the hill as a ball team.

It was over before it had begun. The other teams were able to triple-team and I learned what it is to be a big, marked target.

Also, Bill Russell was halfway towards a swelled head. The newspapers had been good to me. They were picking up some ideas about blocking shots and so forth.

I began to think I was big league. After all, here I was a college sophomore—now earning the princely sum of $30 a month for washing and gassing cars—and getting my name in the papers.

The Swisher girl cut me down to size.

I met my future wife at a dance. She was the niece of Earl Swisher, the man who had been such a good teacher at McClymonds High.

When I was introduced to Rose Swisher, she asked me what I did. I said: "I'm the Bill Russell who plays basketball."

"Where?" she asked. "I never heard of you."

There is nothing like love to bring you down to earth. I stopped reading my press clippings then and haven't saved any since.

USF started getting the clippings in the following

year. We went for all the marbles and it was a crazy, wild sleigh ride that just never stopped.

K.C. Jones was back with us and Jerry Mullen, Stan Buchanan, and Hal Perry were the other starters. We opened against Chico State and beat them 84-55. Creamed Loyola, 54-45. K.C. and I perfected a stunt in that game which we still use to this day. A player was breaking for the basket and had a long lead on us. We couldn't catch him. "I got him, K.C.," I yelled from about ten feet astern. "No, I got him," yelled K.C. from two feet further back.

The poor guy looked over his shoulder and hesitated and missed the basket.

We were going hot, I was hooking, blocking, stuffing shots, making jumpers. Then we ran smack into UCLA which had, among others, a rather stout player named Willie "The Whale" Naulls, an All-American. They lowered the boom. I blew it all by myself. They beat us 47-40.

That was the last one we lost. From there we just took off. Fifty-five straight victories. We ran away and hid from them. We turned them every way but loose. There is no point in going through a lengthy recount of every game we played and everything we did. I stress the we, for regardless of what people said, it was a team effort. It was not just Bill Russell, although at a full 6-10 now, I was the focal point.

We went on to the NCAA finals after winning our regionals. The finals were at Kansas City and it was the first time USF had ever played in a big tournament outside of California, except for the regionals.

I had a new shot now. "The "steer shot" they called it. Somebody would shoot from the outside and if it was a little low I would give a hike and steer it in.

We played LaSalle, starring Tommy Gola, in the finals. Forget it, baby. They weren't going to stop us by this point. K.C. and I doubleteamed poor Gola and we won the championship. After losing that game to UCLA (we won the return match), USF had gone on to win twenty-five straight—all without a home court.

It was a year which was not without its problems. For one thing, there was the coach, Woolpert.

I was not fond of Woolpert as a coach, but I liked him as a man . . . sometimes. I believed then and I believe now that he played favorites. I think he injured the team in the manner in which he played his favorites both during the practice sessions and in the games.

I do not believe Woolpert did this because of prejudice. It was just the way he was. Perhaps it was my own prejudice. But though I gained my first fame with him, I could never be close to him as a man.

I was a good basketball player. There were some who said I was great.

Woolpert never said anything. He never once in all the years said that I did a good job, a bad job, or a mediocre job. I finally mentioned this years later and a wire service sent the story around the country.

Woolpert wrote back a letter saying that he never praised me because I had too much going for me to need that sort of thing. The hell I didn't. Anyone wants to be told they are doing a good job. Anyone wants the support of his coach and this is a lesson coaches should learn in any sport and at any level. It never hurts to say a good word for your player.

It hurt me plenty that Woolpert didn't. And the sore festered even more when—after we had won twenty straight and were headed East for the regionals—Kenny Sears of Santa Clara, whom we had beaten, was named Player of the Year in our conference.

Sears won it strictly because his coach, Bob Feerick, lobbied for him. He constantly said things about Sears at press luncheons. He promoted him as the top professional choice of that year. Woolpert remained silent. All he really had to ask was: "Who won?" But he said nothing.

He was also silent about our great assistant coach, Ross Guidice, who also coached the freshmen. Much of what I am, I owe to Ross, who has since retired and gone into the furniture business in San Francisco. Ross asked nothing of me, except good basketball, and he worked with me throughout my freshman year, playing one-on-one, straightening me out on certain elements of the game—the proper way to take a hook shot, how to play the pivot. He showed great patience and this carried over into the years when we became national champions.

Yet, when we gained this national prominence and the round of banquets and testimonials began, Woolpert never thought to thank Guidice, which hurt him terribly. Woolpert would thank his wife, the dean, this person and that person. But never his assistant, who did so much.

A strange man.

I can never believe he was prejudiced, yet in those days I felt certain that he was. In my freshman year a player named Carl Lawson was starting guard on the varsity. He had earned the job. Now, the next season, a white boy named Rich Moore rejoined the team and Woolpert automatically gave him Lawson's starting job. He didn't even have to earn it. Lawson was shaken. So were we.

In my junior year it happened again. Hal Perry was a starter. Along came Bill Bush and he automatically became the starter. He didn't have to fight for the job. Perry was heart-broken.

It carried over into other areas as well. We had always elected captains. K.C. Jones would have received an almost unanimous vote, but for the first time Woolpert appointed a captain, a player whom I held in low regard, Jerry Mullen. "It will be good for Mullen," Woolpert said.

The next year we went back to elections and K.C. won the honor to which he was entitled.

All of this was desperately important and there is a parallel here, a guideline for any coach in any sport. I don't think to this day Woolpert knows what he did wrong. But a Negro player often assumes he is being put down without a fair chance and, when he runs into a situation which does not seem fair, he does not completely comprehend it and figures that he is being jobbed.

Sometimes he is. Sometimes he is not. But many good players have been destroyed by an unthinking coach who does not recognize that the problem exists.

Now, I had learned something about the name of the game.

33

I also learned something about the collegiate gentlemen who make the rules of the game. I was Most Valuable Player in the NCAA finals when we beat LaSalle and Tom Gola. When the vote went around the country, the Player of the Year was Tom Gola.

It hurt. It seemed like an injustice. Perhaps I made too much of it. It was good practice, anyway, because I learned more about this kind of thing when I switched to the NBA.

If all this sounds like sour grapes, let me say that I have grown tired of sports biographies in which everyone is a dogooder and everything is sugar and spice. It wasn't for me. It wasn't for a lot of others and writing is just like playing the game. Either you tell the truth as you see it, just as you play your guts out, or you shouldn't be in it.

The other thing I learned was more humorous. In this big season I had developed two shots to go with my stuff and block. These were the steer-in and a backwards stuff which I first used against Colorado in the NCAA semifinals.

Athletic directors and coaches around the country immediately sat down and tried to figure out if anything illegal was being done. They couldn't find any violation in the rule book. So, they made up a new rule. The foul lane had been only six feet wide. They lengthened it to twelve feet, supposedly to give faster men a chance. At USF we were laughing. Lengthening the foul lane didn't have anything to do with it and we knew it. It only helped on defense, because it spread them out more. It was called the "Bill Russell Rule" and it couldn't have been better had I written it myself.

During the summer, I decided to go out for track. Actually, I decided it for a dual season. Only varsity lettermen received a button-down sweater. I needed a button-down sweater. The second reason was that I liked to run and jump.

I settled on high jumping, although my other speeds were good enough to make me think of some future decathlon, and in the course of my jumping I became good enough to compete in my senior year against Charlie Dumas, who was heading towards seven feet.

I also made some good friends, among them Johnny Mathis, now better known for his singing. At the time, Mathis was at San Francisco State and competing in the jumping. A whole bunch of us used to climb in an old 1941 Packard I had bought and drive from meet to meet.

That's where I began finding out about the sanctimonious persons—those died-in-the-wool amateurs—the AAU officials, who throw men out of sports for taking two cents.

They should know better. They offer a lot more than two cents. If you are any good and will draw at the gate, they'll pay you right down the line under the guise of expense money.

I know because they tried it on me several times, including the Compton Relays. I didn't know whether I was going or not and a man grabbed me after I tied Dumas at 6-9½ at Fresno and said: "All right. Name your price."

I said: "I don't have any price. I just don't know if I want to go."

"Never mind the sanctimonious bit. Just tell us what it costs," he said.

"Forget it," I answered. "If I come, it will be for the legitimate expense money."

As a matter of fact, I went. I received $6 plus plane fare. The very people who were offering me money had just barred Wes Santee for getting caught taking some. Figure that one.

We had a lot of fun anyway. Mathis never even had expense money. Sometimes I'd get as much as $15 to go to a meet. We'd take a lunch. Now, Mathis could buy the stadium.

There are some great stories about amateur track.

Like the runner who used to get $1 a yard. He was a distance runner. He went to one meet and the promoters showed up $54 short. So he ran anyway. But exactly fifty-four yards from the finish he pulled up lame.

This same man told me he averaged $12,000 a year —tax free—from track. The easiest way for these guys to do it is, let's say, to live in California. Now, they head out for the winter track circuit in the East. They may run in Philadelphia, New York, Boston, Washington on successive weekends. But they demand that they be paid plane-fare from L.A. to the point of the track meet— round trip first class passage.

Then they just drive on to the next town.

A pretty good bit, even though they come up fifty-four yards short once in awhile.

But let's not fake each other out, baby. If it's a profession, then let the corruptors who made it a profession not ruin the young ones whom they corrupt. And they do. They impose one infraction for which the most severe penalties can be exacted—getting caught. Get caught and you're dead.

Meanwhile, they run around in their blazers telling everyone that all they think of is the sport.

Yeah. So do bookmakers.

There's a comparison here somewhere.

You could get a good education at USF. The Jesuits have a flair for it. From all of it, one single instance stands out most in my mind.

It was a class in logic. The priest was leading us down a path of thought when I suddenly realized what he was doing and yelled:

"Hey."

He smiled and said: "Congratulations, Mr. Russell. You have just had your first real and complete thought. How does it feel?"

I never forgot the lesson he taught me.

Think.

During that summer, I received a call from the school saying that I had a letter from the White House.

Much has been said about that. The truth of the matter is I didn't get the letter for three days because it took $1.50 worth of gas and fifty cents toll to cross the bridge to the school and I didn't have the money.

Finally, we scraped it up and went over. It was an invitation to a physical fitness meeting at the White House in July. I would have had to refuse, but USF provided

36

the money and I drove across country with my dad, step-mother, and Rose. I've never been so well-chaperoned in my whole life.

I was representing college basketball at the luncheon. Gene Tunney, Ford Frick, Willie Mays, Hank Greenberg and Bob Cousy were among those present. I didn't even get to talk to Cousy at that time, other than to say a perfunctory hello.

A lot of stories have since come out of that meeting, about President Eisenhower asking me not to turn pro and to play on the Olympic team.

Actually, he never asked me anything about it. Supposedly, I only agreed because the President asked me. That's a nice fable and that's how athletes get rated as nice guys, but the truth is that he didn't ask and if he had I would have told him I didn't know what I was going to do.

In fact, the President just was sort of among those present at the meeting. Somebody read a long report on physical fitness and said the youth of America couldn't even do ten push-ups. To myself I thought: "That's nothing, I can't either."

That was the full extent of the meeting.

From there we went to Louisiana to visit our relatives and for the first time as an adult I came to understand an issue which I would—and will—fight for the remainder of my life.

It was great that I could be a national champion. It was great that I could meet the President of the United States in the White House.

But from Washington to Louisiana and all the way back across the Deep South I was just another black boy, just so much dirt, with no rights, with no element of human courtesy or decency shown to me or mine.

It made an impression. A deep one. It made one that may have affected the rest of my days.

Yet, even this had its humor. On the trip south, we pulled into a gas station in Mississippi and some red-neck came out to wait on us. We had a college sticker on the back window: USF.

"What's that stand for you-all got on the window?" he asked.

"United States Federal," my father said.

The red-neck grinned. "Yep. Ah figured y'all was Federal people."

Our opponents—the red-neck "intellectuals."

Back at USF, the "Homeless Dons" were constructing a gymnasium at last. The campus was growing. The national champions were everyone's target.

But no one could stop us. We ran roughshod over everyone and in December moved into college's real big time, the Holiday Festival at Madison Square Garden.

It was my first visit to New York. I was not impressed. I wasn't accustomed to the cold and the snow and I was on the spot again. Everyone wanted to see how I'd make out in the big leagues.

They saw.

We won it.

We kept right on rolling through the rest of the year. The regular season, the regionals, the NCAA, twenty-nine straight.

National champions again.

Now, they were talking about the Olympics and about pro basketball.

Long since, I had made up my mind that if I were going to play anywhere I would like to be with George Mikan at Minneapolis. Long since, I had also made up my mind that I was going to the Olympics in Melbourne, Australia.

The Olympics officials were already pressing me on whether I was going to turn pro, and Abe Saperstein was urging me to go with the Harlem Globetrotters.

We dedicated the gym on the new campus at USF. Just as I had planned, I was not in the graduating class. I had determined back in my sophomore year that I would not make a mockery of my studies and would trim my subjects in order to play basketball. I was sixteen credits shy on graduation, but I had already planned on going back after my first professional year and taking the one semester I needed.

I did it, too, after the Celtics won the world championship in 1957. I went back to dear old USF to complete my scholarship. I planned on waiving the scholarship and paying for the semester as a gesture of good will.

The gesture was unnecessary. No one offered me the remainder of the scholarship. Dear old USF charged me full retail for my tuition. The scholarship, it turned out, was only good while I was playing basketball.

## CHAPTER III

## THE OLYMPICS

I was leaving USF now, moving on. I had my full growth, six feet, ten inches, I was a giant and one day I would learn and suffer like all men who must write or think those words:

"I am a giant."

To me, they are the hardest words in the world to write. It may not seem so to the average person, but when you say you are a giant, you are exposing a whole world of years when people made fun of you or looked askance at you because you were different.

Years of hurt. Years of trying to prove yourself, not just on a basketball court, but in other ways, of struggling to grow into manhood and be—in all things—a man.

In this year, 1956, I was, however, just a giant college basketball player. The professionals were moving in the background. Abe Saperstein of the Harlem Globetrotters was the first. Saperstein has created an image of himself as a patron of the Negro athlete. I never believed it. Years later, something Walter Brown would say confirmed my views.

Saperstein has never been one for keeping his name out of the papers and as USF rolled to another title, he began spouting fantastic financial offers. Ostensibly, Saperstein was willing to pay me $50,000 to pass up the Olympics and join his Globetrotters after graduation.

The big day when Saperstein would talk with me was scheduled while we were playing in Chicago in the Depaul Invitational.

First, K.C. and some of us stopped by his office. Saperstein started off in a fashion which made me draw back from him like he was contaminated. "Is this what he thinks Negroes are?"

His next volley wasn't any better.

Then he told me to consider closely the "social advantages of playing with the Harlem Globetrotters."

Are you kidding me, Saperstein?

Next, he suggested that I meet him later at our hotel and bring my coach to "keep things on the up and up."

Are you really serious, Saperstein?

But I did it. Woolpert, Ross Guidice and I went up to Saperstein's room. Harry Hanna sat between Ross and me.

My mind was closing rapidly. The gate clicked when I sat back on the couch and Hanna started telling Ross and me jokes while Saperstein devoted all his talk to Woolpert.

That did it. If I'm not smart enough to talk to, then I'm too smart to play for him. Besides, I already knew that he wasn't going to give me any $50,000. He started at $15,000 and went to $17,000. Now a $33,000 difference wasn't friendly. I mean, really. First insults to pride and not talking to me and then the most grievous insult of all—no dough. Goodbye, Mr. Saperstein.

I wish I could say that I didn't play for the Globetrotters only because he didn't talk to me man to man, or that I was bound and determined to represent my country in the Olympics because I was a patriot and because I had promised the President.

But, as you're finding out, this is not the friendship diary of a typical American athlete who makes good.

In the first place, I hadn't promised the President anything. Secondly, I had already computed that the Trotters played every night and that even $50,000 would be short money on a per game basis by comparison with what I might get in the pros. And thirdly, I just wanted to go to the Olympics. I had my mind made up.

Years later, I found out that Saperstein threatened Walter Brown—the late owner of the Celtics and the key founder of the league—when Brown was getting ready to sign Chuck Cooper as the first Negro on the

Celtics. Saperstein had the control in those days. His Globetrotters packed them in everywhere they went and the NBA was teetering along on the verge of bankruptcy and needed them at the gate.

Saperstein thought he had a lock on all Negro players. He came at Brown hammer and tongs and told Walter that if the Celtics signed Cooper then the Globetrotters would boycott Boston Garden.

"You won't boycott us," Brown said. "You'll just never get in here again. Nobody threatens me."

That's the kind of man Brown was. At the time, he had run his personal finances down to a big flat zero, had sold his house and some of his furniture, and his own job as President of the Boston Garden was in jeopardy—all because he believed that the Celtics and pro basketball would click.

Later events proved him right. But I think the strain of it all was what caused his early and to us so terribly tragic death of a heart attack, September 7, 1964.

Brown and Red Auerbach of the Celtics had also been working in the background throughout my senior year. I didn't want to play for them. I wanted to play for Minneapolis. Rochester was the bottom team in the league that year, thus having first pick, and Lester Harrison contacted me. I figured I had better give them the deep six because I just couldn't imagine spending the winter in Rochester, New York, so I told him I'd have to have $25,000.

"Well, yep. Don't call us, we'll call you," Lester said and immediately went on to let it be known that they were taking Sihugo Green as their number one draft choice.

I like Lester Harrison. Still do. As an aside, however, there was one thing. When Harrison came to see me, he brought along one of his former players, Dolly King, who was a Negro. Without realizing it, Lester was insulting both King and me. King, apparently, was supposed to let me know that "Lester treats us right." This is a big mistake, practiced by many coaches . . . and many people. Honestly, King couldn't make a difference. One Negro is not automatically going to be the buddy-buddy of the other. It doesn't take one Negro to talk to another.

42

I mean, we all speak English, white or black, right?

Meantime, Auerbach had concocted the trade which might bring the Celtics their first world championship. Strength off the boards.

His first step was to contact Pete Newell of U. of Cal. Newell was asked, secretly:

"Is Russell a team player?

"Can he make it in the NBA? Does he have the guts?"

Auerbach was working far under the surface. The idea was that I would not be aware of what was going on, not know how badly he wanted me and, therefore, not ask for a large salary.

Red, I've got news for you. I knew it all along. My hopes of going to Minneapolis with George Mikan went right out the window. I was checking on Red, as well. I made up my mind that I was going to the Celtics.

Auerbach's next step was another typical cutie. Easy Ed Macauley, the tall, painfully thin Celtics center, was getting killed under the boards. Aging, tired, he wanted to return to his hometown, St. Louis. "Trade me, or I'll quit."

Now Auerbach—who coached for one year for Ben Kerner—phoned his old boss and offered a trade. St. Louis needed a center. He would give them Macauley for their first draft choice. Namely, me.

Kerner, who didn't get rich giving things away, smelled a rat and held Auerbach up in turn. That must have been a phone call to listen to. Here were two guys who were sharp, rough and tough and really hated each other.

Kerner finally got his way. He demanded that Auerbach give him Macauley and a Celtic rookie, Cliff Hagan. Auerbach knew he had to do it and in that trade he knew very well that he was setting up a dog-eat-dog fight in the playoffs of 1957. Just how even that trade turned out to be is shown in the seventh and final game of that world championship series when we went all the way to a second overtime before we finally won it.

Meanwhile, I was just having fun thinking about what it would be like to be rich. The Celtics exercised their agreement with St. Louis and picked me in the May draft, but no one from Boston contacted me.

I was in the middle of getting ready for the Olympics.

Teddy White should write *The Making of the Olympics* some day if he really wants to see politics in action.

That has to be the greatest bit of sugar-'n-spice-in-the-mouth-and-bourbon-in-the-belly-carney-type-conning since Barnum and Bailey. If you put the whole Olympic Committee of 1956 out in the rain with umbrellas, there would only be about three of them with enough sense to open the bumbleshoot and get out of the wet.

In this period, the AAU and NCAA were feuding for power. A deal was made with the Olympic Committee that the basketball team would have five players from the AAU, three from the NCAA and two each from the Army and the Air Force.

You could make some good money in the AAU. Some companies sponsor teams, such as the Phillips Oilers, Goodyear and Vickers Petroleum. Conceivably, this could be considered a public-spirited enterprise to assist the Olympics. Perhaps the companies think so.

I was offered $500 to play in a pre-Olympic trial AAU Tournament for the Vickers team. I turned it down to go with the NCAA team for $2 a day expenses. Reason? Let's just say the AAU and I are never going to agree on athletics.

The Olympic trials in basketball are divided into sections. The AAU team, the NCAA team—known as the College All Stars—and the military teams of the Army and Air Force.

In the tournament I ran across dishonest officiating for the first time. I thought it was incompetence at first, but then I saw that this was fully intended to strengthen the hand of the AAU. They succeeded. Everyone else was shafted and I feel this even though I was selected. The Phillips Oilers won the tourney and their starting five were picked. Carl Cain of Iowa, K.C. Jones and Russell made it from the College All Stars. Willie Naulls of UCLA and Hal Lear of Temple were among those who didn't have a chance of making the team.

I thought at the time that only three Negroes were selected because of prejudice, but as I look back on it, politics was the answer, not prejudice. Lear, for exam-

44

ple, played better than Cain. However, Cain's coach, the late Bucky O'Connor of Iowa, was doubling as the coach of the College All Stars in the pre-Olympic trials. So Cain was the choice.

Cain, incidentally, has a lovely sister, Beverly, and K.C. Jones is now married to her. I liked Cain. I liked Lear. But I felt there was undue influence exerted here.

The team having been picked, we were now taken to training camp and on tour. It was a massive series of incidents. The Olympic Committee warned us not to make any statements which might be embarrassing to the United States, either in our own country or when we reached the Olympics.

Then they proceeded to place us in situation after situation where we were segregated or embarrassed.

It was a hurting thing. Not desperate. We were men. We had experienced it before. But for all three of us, it was another scar, another slice. We were representing our nation in the largest sports event in the world. But in our home country we were not equal as citizens.

Their warning, however, was unnecessary. We were, after all, Americans. Our battleground was in the United States, not as pawns to the publicity endeavors of the Communist press.

They always take the Olympic basketball team on tour to raise money for the trip. They don't have to raise much for the athletes. All they take is eleven players. Then they flush the rest of it out with public relations directors, travel co-ordinators, counselors, etc. Funny, but it always seems to wind up that the last named are the ones who need extra funds for entertainment and side trips for cultural exchange and big suites in hotels. So the Olympic team played exhibitions.

We wound it up in Washington, D.C., and I wound up coming into Washington with a hernia.

"Don't worry," the little-souled man from the Olympic Committee—oh, I wish I could remember his name —told me. "We've got to have you to get the Gold Medal. But after that we'll pay for your operation because you hurt it working for us."

45

In Washington I played the poorest game I'd had in years. Auerbach was watching me for the first time.

Afterwards, he took me home for dinner. He looked a little green. "Look," I said. "I don't usually play quite that bad."

Auerbach shrugged. "If you do," he said, "you better stay in Melbourne because I won't be in Boston. I'll be back coaching junior high in Brooklyn."

Not too much of that meeting comes back, except that Auerbach made a heckova more honest impression than some of the people I'd been meeting in the past few years. I had a hunch he was more interested in people than just hunks of beef in short pants.

Auerbach's offer was acceptable. I was to receive $22,500. Since I would be gone for the first two months of the season, I would take a $6000 cut in salary.

We had a gentleman's agreement that I would sign when I returned home and would report after I married Rose in December.

We prepared for Melbourne. I had an offer to play "amateur" basketball in Europe for $15,000 and an all-expenses stay in Italy. The $15,000 was to be put on deposit for me in the City Bank and Trust of New York and I could still keep my amateur standing.

I turned it down. Now I was in great shape. I said "no" to Saperstein's $17,000. I turned down Vickers' $500. I waved off $15,000 from the Italian amateurs and I was taking a $6000 cut in salary from the Celtics.

And I had a hernia.

I mean, how much can you give for your country?

While waiting for the trip, we took a quick State Department swing to South America. Willie Naulls went along, I guess as sort of a sop to him for being gypped out of the Olympics. (Remember, now, remember this, you who read this and say I am talking out of a Negro's anger. He was gypped out of the Olympics because of politics, not because he was a Negro. Another Negro, Cain, had taken his place.)

We returned to Los Angeles and were booked to fly to Melbourne when Avery Brundage came after me. "If he intends to turn professional, then he violates the ethics of amateurism. He should guarantee he will continue as an amateur or he shouldn't compete in the Olympics," said the man who has sown so much confusion in amateur athletics.

Some people wanted me to quit.

Not so.

I said: "I'm more of an amateur than anyone on the Committee, or any other athlete on the teams. You'll have to kick me out. I won't quit."

I made the trip. My hernia, my $72 spending money, and me. Two hours out of Hawaii the plane caught fire.

Well, sir, if you're going to argue with Avery Brundage this is the chance you have to take.

Oh, my God. Sick? Scared? Upset? Tense? Are you kidding me, baby? We were 20,000 feet over the Pacific and the flames were coming back over the wing and the outboard engine was clearly about to depart us.

Fortunately, we had a great pilot. It was a Pan American plane. Maybe it was the same one who made that jet landing in San Francisco in 1965. Or his twin brother. The pilot did a fantastic job of bringing us home to Hawaii and we waited eight hours and went off again. In the same plane, incidentally.

This time we reached Melbourne. It was the last of October and the Olympics were about to start.

It was one of the biggest thrills of my life. I had a wonderful time. We all mingled together, even the Russians, whom we beat by thirty-five points.

The Russians couldn't speak English, but they must have been told to be on their good behavior. There was one little guy—oh, about 6-2—who played opposite me and all he would do was smile and raise his hands over his head to show me how much taller I was. We went through them in salty fashion—Russia, Thailand, Philippines, Uruguay, Japan—and we won the Gold Medal.

Swimmer Dawn Fraser has had a lot to say about her view of extra fun and games among the Olympians, but I must confess I saw none of that in her native Australia . . . and it wasn't because I didn't look. The only ones who were strange were the U.S. Gymnasts. They didn't talk to anyone and stayed by themselves, but

47

when they went into competition they didn't have much to talk about anyway.

Speaking of good behavior, I wish I could say as much for the Olympic officials. For them it was like one mammoth old boys' convention. The only time we saw them was when it was time to take pictures. For the rest, they were on one big round of parties.

This is not a vendetta against the United States Olympic Committee. But over the years I have discovered that it is a climate such as this which creates our failure as athletes in international competition. Too many of our athletes know this and refuse to say anything because they are afraid of the action which might be taken.

They couldn't keep their word on anything. Before we left the country—oh, way back in August—I had told them I was getting married on December 9 in Oakland, California.

The first planes were due to leave on December 6. The travel coordinator had assured me I would be on it. But now the Olympic Committee members all had to be on the first plane home and I wouldn't be getting out until the tenth—one day after my wedding date.

I screamed so loud they could hear me back in Oakland. I received a seat.

I came back with the Harvard rowing team and sat with Jack Kelly, the Philadelphian whose sister is Princess Grace. A fine guy and we had a wonderful conversation over the next twenty-four hours as we headed for home. I was too embarrassed to mention his sister.

Home for me was a total of forty-one sleepless hours away and I arrived in Oakland just in time to make the wedding rehearsal at the Taylor Methodist Church.

I asked the Reverend how many the church would hold and he assured us that it had never been filled. The wedding the next day had an overflow crowd of 300. We had a police escort to the reception in San Francisco. One summer before, I hadn't had the fifty cents toll to go across the Bay Bridge to get a letter from the President. Now the police took me over like I was the Mayor—or like I was bound for San Quentin on the other side.

We honeymooned in Carmel and seven days later we were on a plane bound for Boston. I still hadn't signed, but I knew I would. My amateur days were behind me and I had an Olympic Gold Medal. And a hernia.

I must tell you the sequel to that hernia, for which the Olympians insisted they would pay.

After the first Celtic world championship I contacted the Olympic team physician, Dr. Brick Mueller, who referred me to the main office in Chicago.

The response was terse:

"The Olympic Committee cannot pay for the cost of this operation because you have become a professional."

The true, blue sportsmen to the very, very, end.

# CHAPTER IV

## CAST OF CHARACTERS

Now it began. The loneliest life in the world. A world of bright lights and screaming emotion and vast amounts of money—and deep wells of loneliness. So deep. Such an abyss. You fall far into it and all your life struggle to come back up.

Perhaps only the people who have been privileged and damned by being what society calls a super star can know it. Perhaps it is just part of the American culture.

Yet, have you ever noticed that there have been few super stars who managed to survive the pressure? They have all felt it. Mays. Mantle. Cobb. Williams. Cousy. Patterson . . . Russell.

Now, never knowing whether I would make it or not, I was stepping into that world, into a cast of characters who would over the years become a strong force in my life.

The Celtics.

Seven lonely months of hotel rooms and airplanes and violence and more hotel rooms and chicanery and confusion and card games and card-sharks and more hotels and more airplanes and more of the violence of two hundred pound men slashing away at each other for a valued prize—the money that goes only to the champion.

When I first came to them, they were at last on the move toward the championship which had so long eluded them. I was not the most welcome sight ever to appear in the dressing room. For one thing, I was unproven. They were two months into the season and they were leading the league and many people said that Russell couldn't make the league. "Russell doesn't have the shot to be a pro," the writers said.

One of the few times I agreed with them.

The only thing I knew was that there was more to this game than shooting a basketball.

And no one was going to drive me out. I was in, baby. Yeah, Jack, I was in to stay.


We arrived on a cold December afternoon. Snow and slush. I was met by the late Walter Brown, who owned the Celtics and was the founder of the NBA. At the time he was flirting along the edges of bankruptcy. I was supposed to sign a contract for $22,500—minus the six grand which I lost for going to the Olympics.

Brown said: "Hell, why should I punish you for winning a Gold Medal. I'll split the difference with you. Sign for $19,500."

Thus I became a Celtic. From that moment to the day of his death, I never had an argument about money with Walter Brown—or any argument at all. He asked me each year what I wanted and I told him and he said: "Sign."

I was a Celtic at last. Let's consider for a minute what I was becoming, joining this league of strange giants. The NBA was still a bush league in those days, a "little" league. One of its few consistent leaders was Brown.

He was the last of the true sportsmen and the true secret of the success of the Celtics stemmed from his spirit. He wasn't always right. But he was always a man.

Long before basketball, he had been a hockey fan. As a kid, he took AAU teams to Europe. When I rapped AAU and Olympic officials, I was not including those who were cast in the mold of Brown. He was an authentic sportsman.

Brown literally formed the NBA. He was President of the Boston Garden, President of the Boston Bruins, a Director of Ice Capades, Ice Follies, ran the BAA Marathon. In the summer of 1945 he was walking down Fifth Avenue on his way to the annual Arena Managers meeting with two sports editors, Sam Cohen of the then Boston *Daily Record* and Max Kaese of the New York *Journal-American*. They suggested the possibility of a professional basketball league and Brown said: "It sounds reasonable. Let's do it."

He walked into the Commodore Hotel and put it before the Arena Managers. John Harris of Pittsburgh said: "If you're in, Walter, so am I." Lester Harrison of Rochester agreed. It went around the table. Walter was in. The NBA was formed.

There were years after that when everyone wished it had died at birth. In Boston it laid a particularly big egg.

Brown was a hockey buff. It was his greatest love. But he was a sportsman too. He wouldn't believe the sport couldn't survive and he poured every single dime he had into it. He lost every cent. The Boston Garden decided to discontinue basketball, so Brown bought the team himself. His money went and went and went.

This has to be the greatest story in the history of professional sports. One man and a few friends going against the tide, refusing to pack it in, and winding up with the greatest world championship streak on record.

Remember this, if you are ever going to play professional sports. It is just that. A profession. A big time business and a player is only a hunk of meat on the block and good for only so long before spoilage sets in.

Only men like Brown ever take it out of the realm of mediocrity.

And only his faith sustained him. American Airlines once carried him on a bill which would have bought them a small airplane because they knew he was good for it.

Some fantastic stories can be told about him, and should be, because this is the inner story of how a world champion was made.

Eddie Powers, now the Garden President, was the Treasurer then. He lived and feared and battled alongside Brown. But one day the coffers were dry.

"How much do you need to keep going?" Brown asked.

"It's a nightmare," Powers said. "The government men were in to collect back taxes and threatened foreclosure. I told them to go ahead. I said: 'Great. We have ten ball players who can't do anything but play basketball and have absolutely no value on a tax return.

" 'But we have a few assets. We have two bottles of aspirin, four rolls of tape and ten used jockstraps. And two basketballs that could use a little inflation. Close the joint up. Put the lock on the door. See what you can get for our assets.'

"That's how bad things are, Walter."

Brown dug around in his desk and came up with a bank book.

"This is the end of it, Eddie," he said. "This is get-away money. I've been saving this $5000 for the last day. It's the end of my life's savings."

They went to the bank and Powers tells a wonderful story about presenting the book. A CPA, Powers is a genius with figures and he noted that the interest was nearly due. He computed that a loan against the book would result in $41 extra payment within twelve days, so he began negotiating the deal.

Brown fidgeted from one foot to the other. Finally he said: "For heaven's sakes, Eddie. Here I am blowing the last five gees I have in the world and you're arguing about $41. Get the execution over with, will you?"

They paid two bills with the five thou' and they were right back where they started again. It was so bad that after they made the playoffs Brown still didn't have the playoff shares to pay Cousy and Sharman. The latter pair were broke themselves, but they just said: "Okay, Walter, don't worry. You're good for it."

Brown couldn't keep going and everyone knew it. He contacted five moneymen and offered them one half the team at $5,000 apiece. The moneymen turned it down. The Celtics were dead.

But word reached Lou Pieri, owner of the Providence Auditorium. "I'm in for twenty-five big ones and a draw up to $100,000," Pieri said, "but you have to agree to get Red Auerbach to be your coach."

Auerbach didn't have a gentle reputation, but Brown was in no position to argue.

Auerbach arrived in Boston. It was 1950.

To show you how the luck of the draw goes, Auerbach was fired by Ben Kerner and was about finished with the pros. Pieri was holding pretty good, but was not enormously wealthy. Brown had nothing.

He hired Auerbach. In 1964, when Walter Brown died, L. Pieri was already the winner of over half a million dollars, Auerbach was owner of ten percent of the team and on his way to being a millionaire in his own right, and Brown's estate was over $1,000,000. It worked out well for all three and it worked out well for Cousy and me, among others.

In fact, after Brown died in 1964, Pieri represented the estate in a deal to sell the team. He finally sold it to Ruppert-Knickerbocker for $3,000,000, of which Auerbach got $300,000, Pieri $1,300,000, and Brown's widow, Marjorie, $1,300,000.

Moral—courage can pay off if you are a man like Brown. Sports can pay off if you are a man like Auerbach. It pays to have $25,000 to invest if you are a man like Pieri.

The story has often been told of how Auerbach "got stuck" with Bob Cousy. Auerbach never did have a winning personality and when he came to Boston he succeeded in alienating the press and the fans by putting the rap on Cousy who had been their All-American hero from Holy Cross and who was drafted by Tri-Cities, which was now about to become St. Louis.

Three players were in the hat. The Celtics wanted either Max Zaslofsky or Andy Phillip, not Cousy. The owners sat around yelling at each other in the Commodore Hotel in New York. Finally, Brown took the hat off Danny Biasone's head and said "Here. Put the three names in there and we'll draw for them."

Then, being the polite man he was, he offered the other two teams first pick. They picked Phillip and Zaslofsky. That left Cousy.

And the door to the world championship swung open.

When it came to me, Auerbach pulled his switch on Kerner, so that's twice he got old lovable Ben. As Brown told me the story later, he didn't want to go with it at first, but Auerbach insisted and so the deal was made. Brown really loved Ed Macauley who was the nice, skinny, clean-living center who was traded to St.

Louis. He wound up with nice, skinny, goateed, I-won't-go-into-the-clean-living-bit me.

That's how the stage was set as I arrived in Boston, a team which had had a Negro player (Chuck Cooper), but no longer had any.

Cousy and Sharman were in the backcourt, triggering the fast break. Rookie Heinsohn was at one forward, Arnie Risen at center, Jim Loscutoff on the other corner. Leading subs were Jack Nichols, Dick Hemric and a whiffle-haired Army veteran named Frank Ramsey—All-American at Kentucky—and the "sixth man."

Then they got me.

I was less worried about how they would accept me than I was about how I would accept them.

Some, players and fans, were certain to judge me on race. I had two strikes going. I was a 6-10 giant. I was a Negro. The combination provided the bigots with plenty of material for sly jokes.

I told Rose then and there that I knew regardless of how well I might do—and most writers were saying that I wouldn't make it—I would never be a legitimate sports hero in Boston or anywhere else.

I had the feeling. It was partly just me. I had made up my mind that I would not become the bigot's stereotype of the Negro. I would not be the laughing boy, seeking their favors. I would just be me. Take it any way you want to.

There were some who expected me to curry favor with them. I had news for them, baby. I didn't and I won't. I wrote some controversial articles, but I believed them at the time. I was talking human rights before it was popular.

Later, some views would of necessity change. This is a matter of situation and experience.

But to thine ownself be true. Yeah, Jack, to thine ownself be true.

I immediately liked Sharman, who was among those who met us at the airport. And I was attached to Arnie Risen, the aging star who would leave us after one more year. I was taking Risen's job and I would not have blamed him if he had hated me.

Instead, Arnie Risen went out of his way to help. I've

never forgotten him for it and I never will. Remember, this was professional sports and the money was on the line. Risen transcended the norm for a professional sportsman. He was a team man all the way.

I never had much to do with Bob Cousy. Don't misunderstand what I say—I'm not faulting the greatness of Bob Cousy.

We were roommates on one trip to New York and I never wanted to room with him again. Not for any personal reasons. It was just that I like to sleep in the afternoon before a game. Cooz went out of the hotel and I started trying to sleep and it was as if he was the majority stockholder in American Tel and Tel. The phone rang thirty-one times before he came back.

When he finally returned he received a call and he talked French for forty-seven minutes. I figured it was an overseas call. But at the end he said: "Okay, Momma. See you soon," and hung up.

Cooz, as you may not know, didn't even speak English until he was five years old and that is why he has that accent of his. He was born right in New York and never saw grass until he was ten and moved to Long Island and he never could make his high school basketball team until he was a senior. I guess there was a parallel of sorts there between us.

In later years, as the pressure built up, Cousy went through the torture that only a super star can really know.

The lot of the super star is—lonely nights, horrible hotel rooms, and nightmares. There is the story Cousy tells about his nightmares and sleepwalking that got so bad he eventually had to tie himself to his bed. Cousy's nightmares were so terrifying he once got out of bed stark naked and wound up dashing himself against trees as he ran from his frightening dream—and this was off-season.

When you think about the glory of being a super star, of being a really famous star in a sport, add a dash of this kind of thing. I've had it myself, although mine developed into insomnia and almost a nervous breakdown. It is partly the man and partly the pressure of professional sports.

In our own personal relationship, Cousy and I shared a locker-room, airplanes, hotels, cars, cabs, a team for six years, but we just never seemed to be able to initiate anything other than a few passing comments.

It was not dislike, but rather a mutual respect. I thought he was a superb player. Apparently he thought I was pretty good, and we were in the unusual circumstance of almost being competitors for the role of key to the Celtics' string of world championships.

I would get things like this. You've just played a game and you've blocked fourteen shots, scored twenty-three points and grabbed thirty-one rebounds against somebody like Chamberlain and the Celtics are now one up in the Eastern finals and you come out of the dressing room door and someone says: "Let me shake your hand. I've just shaken the hand of the greatest basketball player in the world, Bob Cousy. Now, I want to shake the hand of the second greatest."

Of course you take a slow burn. It's perfectly normal. And I know Cousy did, too, because he had some of the same experiences.

Yet, I had—and do have—a tremendous affinity for Cooz and I would like to think he shares it. At 6-10 I'm only average nowadays as centers go, or even a small guy, compared with some others in this league. Cousy was only 6-1 and he brought great appeal to basketball because the fans could identify with him—a little man, an average man, not some giant, some freak as they sometimes call us.

The Cooz could do some fantastic things for a little man amid giants. When it ended, after six world championships, we had something deep and close and unspoken and I felt and feel that we will be friends for life.

Cousy's buddy was rookie Tommy Heinsohn. Heinsohn—the "Hawk," the "Gunner"—played against me in the Holiday Tournament in Madison Square Garden when he was center for Holy Cross.

Now we were teammates and he was playing magnificent pro basketball. We were both rookies, but somehow Heinsohn was the only one receiving a rookie's hazing. Like carrying the sound machine on trips, or getting the tea ready. All the routine hazings that go with being a rook.

I was never asked to run out for a Coke, or to carry the trainer's bag.

On the surface, the team didn't appear to need me. They were going strong, leading the league.

Auerbach said he knew what he was doing. I knew what I was doing. I was going to go out and play my guts out and prove a point. To me. Just to me. In all my life, I've never done anything I didn't do flat out—right or wrong—and I don't know any other way to do it.

I cannot say that I was particularly close to anyone on that first championship team. I was the interloper, the factor that they needed to make the mathematical problem spell world championship. But I had a small chip on my shoulder and I was coming in halfway through their season, which didn't add anything to team camaraderie.

Ramsey was from Kentucky and he has since become one of my dearest and most respected friends. Ramsey was always known as the "Best Sixth Man in Basketball." He won the nom de court the hard way. There is nothing more difficult than coming into a game without any warmup and playing either the corner or the backcourt for four minutes full tilt and then going out again. A good sixth man can provide the spurt that wins—and, as a matter of fact, it was Ramsey who won our first world championship for us under pressure.

"Rams" had just come out of the Army after playing four great years at Kentucky. Just before he went into the Army he joined the Celtics and they played a road game somewhere and, as was traditional at that time, they lost. Risen found Ramsey sitting in a corner completely discouraged and disconsolate. "What's the matter, kid?" Risen asked.

"I never lost a game before," Ramsey said.

"Stick around here. You'll get used to it," Risen said.

But Ramsey never did. He was in his element only when he came back to the Celtics and the team started winning.

When Auerbach began talking retirement the natural coaching choice was Frank.

It is perhaps strange to think that Ramsey—a white Kentuckian—would be a friend, but there has never been any clique according to color on the Celtics and this was another reason for our success.

But there was a quota in the NBA and I said so. I said there was an unwritten law of pro basketball that no team should have more than two Negroes—three at the most—because in the opinion of the owners it would be bad for a draw at the gate—and money, not heart, rules pro sports.

I was right about it, too. When I brought it out in the open, Brown told me: "I never looked at the color of a player in my life. You tell me where the good players are and I'll take them, green, purple, brown, black, white or peppermint."

I believe he meant it, but the fact remained that there was still an even distribution on all teams. It took a long time before the Negro was ever truly accepted in pro basketball. Now, there is no quota and I would like to think that I had at least something to do with it by sounding off about it when it was an unpopular thing to do.

Later it was pointed out to me—many times—that in the year I spoke up, there were six Negroes in the starting ten members on the All Star team.

The pointers missed the point. The issue, you see—you must see—is that a quota starts at the bottom, not at the top.

Ramsey, though a Southerner, is a sensible, sane human being and I always felt that it was men like Frank who could help us solve our joint problems in this complex society.

For myself, I felt that I was never going to be well-loved, or even well-liked, but I was going to fight the problem out all the way. There were some hurts and I gave some hurts back, but at this time—which was before the civil rights movement really got popular—I was saying things which I think were later borne out.

We did have some cracks between the races on the Celtics. Perhaps the funniest happened years later when

Ramsey was put into a game with Sam Jones, K.C. Jones, Tom Sanders and me. We played for about two minutes and were far ahead when Ramsey scored a few points. Rams came back to the bench with us at the next time out and said to Auerbach and all of us:

"Hey, Red. What am ah, the white hope?"

Rams was our accountant. He could tell you anything about taxes, interest, mortgages. He was also our fiercest competitor. He coined a saying before our first world championship in the dead stillness of our locker-room before the seventh and final game and it became traditional ever after.

We were waiting to go out and I was just coming from casting away my supper and standing in the doorway and Cousy was sitting with his head down. Auerbach was chewing the bottom off a dead cigar and puffing it absentmindedly not realizing it wasn't lit and Heinsohn was prowling back and forth from wall to wall.

Ramsey just sat there. Then as the knock came on the door—the moment that you dread and love all wrapped up in one—Rams said:

"You all listen now. You all playin' with mah money. Don't y'all make any mistakes."

Ramsey always figured out how we whacked up the playoff money as well and he had a marvelous sense of humor and timing. Just before that first world championship series opened with St. Louis, Auerbach was in a bad mood and was snarling at us in a practice session. "You're not worth the money," he said to the team.

Ramsey turned to him and said on behalf of all of us: "Hey, Red. You're so great? How many world championships did you ever win before we got here?"

To Auerbach's credit, he broke up.

Ramsey was great at drawing fouls from an opponent. He developed the fallaway routine where an official making a judgment call would turn and catch Rams falling out of the corner of his eye and immediately grab the nearest opponent for pushing. Rams—if you played by the regulations—was also a "Cutie" in the sense that he knew just how to tug, push, shove and get away with it.

But he never purposely hurt anyone, which in the pros is the real criterion. He suffered many injuries himself and he used to play in agony sometimes, wrapped up like a mummy from toe to thigh. But he always played.

Rams has a speech impediment, a stutter which led to the best practical joke in the history of the Celtics.

He went into a restaurant in a hotel with Sharman and ordered: "Tw-two Cokes."

We'd already bribed the girl and she brought him four—two and two. Rams just sat and looked at her and looked and looked and finally she came back and he said: "I ordered tw-two Cokes," so she said:

"That's what I brought you. Two and two. Four cokes."

We didn't cure him of stuttering, but he never went back to that coffee shop, either.

Every time Rams made an investment it seemed to turn out golden. Over the years, everyone tried to get a piece of a deal. Finally, in 1962, Ramsey researched a plan to breed chickens. Loscutoff and Auerbach were among the big investors.

Ramsey went home for the off season and Loscie sat around waiting to count his money. The next thing he received from Kentucky was a clipping of the Madisonville *Gazette* which headlined: TORNADO STRIKES MADISONVILLE. The story went on to say that fortunately the storm hit only the outskirts and just one building was damaged. "Frank Ramsey's chickenhouse was blown away."


Loscutoff is the next in the increasing cast of the characters who made the Celtics great.

Loscie weighed in at 230 pounds and stood 6-5. He was an All-American at Oregon and was starting in the other corner when I came aboard.

His real job was to be our policeman. He was known as the league's bullyboy and wherever we went Loscie's muscles went with us up until his last year, 1963.

Jim was Heinsohn's roommate. Heinsohn loved to tell the story of the time he came into the room and found Loscutoff doing one of those Charles Atlas poses in front of the mirror. He looked up at Heinie and said: "Gee, no wonder my wife loves me. I'm beautiful."

Heinie never let him forget that one.

As a player, Loscutoff had his hands full. He came along in the league at a time when the accent was switching from the real tough guys to speed and shooters with the "cops" on the sideline.

He didn't play too much and he suffered a slipped disc early in the 1959-60 season. The doctors said he would never play basketball again.

With the help of our trainer, Buddy LeRoux, he was back in shape by September of the following year. It was one of the great examples of a trainer working with an athlete.

Auerbach didn't want to take him back mainly because he felt that if anything happened to cripple Loscutoff it would be his fault.

He treated Loscutoff like a dog during that training period. He once started on Loscutoff to see whether he could make all the moves that might be required of a cornerman.

The practice was over, and we stood around laughing as Auerbach started Loscutoff diving and rolling for balls and yelling: "Fetch . . . fetch . . ." He threw the ball in every imaginable way and after a time we stopped laughing. It was deadly serious business. I wouldn't have blamed Loscutoff if he had stood up and whacked Auerbach in the mouth. He didn't. He hung in there and when they were through, Auerbach had made up his mind that Loscutoff would stay.

There is one great story about Loscie. His style was to play hold and grab, and one night he was guarding George Yardley. Yardley went to break away and Loscutoff was left holding his pants. It was the easiest holding call any ref has ever had to make.

When I first joined the Celts I figured Loscie for a bully. Frankly, I think he was. He liked to test people. I gave him a little lead rope and then I said: "Loscie, it's gonna go one way or the other. You cross me one more time and I'm gonna romp and stomp and turn you every way but loose, baby."

Loscie answered: "Bring your lunch."

I put on my best scowl: "Yeah, and I'll bring my supper too, baby." (And sundry less printable words to that effect. We never had any trouble after that.)

We've had some interesting characters, believe me. We had the steady ones. A couple of choke-up artists. A couple of card sharks. A few lovers—you know, the kind who are chosen "Man of the Year" by the stewardesses of Eastern Airlines; some journeymen just passing through; one or two temperamental ones and, coupled all together, one helluva team for nine solid seasons.

Heinsohn left us in 1965 and undoubtedly one day he will be in the Hall of Fame. But even Tommy will never know how good he could have been.

He had more physical ability than any forward who ever played the game, but in my opinion he never came close to playing to his potential. He thought he didn't have the stamina. But I think he did.

I said one time and I say it again now that Auerbach made one big mistake with Heinsohn. He should have made Heinsohn run until he fell down and then thrown water on him and told him to start running again. Heinie was a great shot with that jumper of his. It was beautiful—a line drive which just went straight in. He learned it as a kid in New Jersey, playing in a small gym with a low ceiling and it was a revolutionary shot in pro basketball.

Heinsohn was also something of a revolutionist. He became our player representative and was deeply involved in representing the request for an insurance plan and a pension fund.

The result of our activities was the players' strike before the 1964 All Star Game when we became disgusted with the doubledealing of the owners and refused to take the floor, even though the game was on national television.

That may have seemed childish, but let me tell you some of the background of dealing with the owners.

Remember, this is a professional business. The owners are in the league to make money. They do not desire to pay the athletes more than they have to. In recent years, the owners, through success and through attrition, have become wealthy men. But, some of them remember, and react to, the old days when they used to drive the bus, collect money by passing a hat, and hustle just about anything on the side to get by.

Part of all the troubles which have beset this league are, I believe, a direct result of a certain lassitude on the part of one particular clique of owners who overlook the fact that they have finally and truly achieved the big league status for which they have so long dreamed and conned and worked and gambled.

But, let this be a true statement about professional sports for any of you who may ever be considering it. Professional sports is a profession. The owners are never going to be in love with you. Never. They're in it to make money and you're in it to make money and never the twain shall fully meet, except occasionally in the tumult and ecstasy of a world championship game.

Even such a great star as Cousy found that out. Cousy was preparing to retire in 1963. There is no doubt that he did more to save the game and more to enhance big league status than any other single man. He was considering an offer to coach Boston College, but he also would have considered an offer to be President of the NBA. The original President, stormy Maurice Podoloff, was retiring at the end of the season.

An exploratory query was made and in his typical honest way, Cousy said:

"I'll take it on one condition—that the owners can't tell me what to do."

This is a job that pays $50,000 a year, so you can see that Cooz has to be a real man to talk that way.

Walter Brown, however, great as he was, couldn't see that. "I'm an owner and I would never have a President who would have free reign," Brown said. "I don't think they'll give it to you anyway, because they never would want a player to be in control. I know they won't go for a President they can't run. We just have too big a stake in this thing. We put in too many years of sweat and money to have anybody now tell us how it should be run."

That was a great man like Walter Brown talking. You can imagine how some of the other owners—who I believe I can say with candor are not exactly reaching to the heights of greatness—would feel.

The league wound up with J. Walter Kennedy replacing Mr. Podoloff. Mr. Kennedy previously was the league publicist when the NBA was formed and then drifted away to become Mayor of Stamford, which for some reason automatically qualified him for the job of President of a major sport.

On several occasions he has been involved in some interesting decisions.

The most interesting of all was this one on the players' pension plan. At best, our union is pretty weak. It is nothing compared to that of baseball. Neither are the salaries, but over the years we managed to get a few concessions: a minimum salary of $7500 for rookies; agreements on playoff schedules.

For three years we requested a modest pension plan. In reply we received the swerve and the stall and the screws.

We continued asking. Finally, they agreed that we would meet in Boston during the All Star Game of 1964. All we wanted was a contributory plan which amounted to $500 from the team and $500 from the player. It was a very modest start, but we felt it could develop.

That afternoon, we went up to the Sheraton-Plaza for our meeting, but we couldn't get all the owners together. Then we went to see J. Walter Kennedy and he promised we would all be able to sit down before the game that night.

Do a slow dissolve now into late afternoon with Heinsohn making phone call after phone call. No answer. Tommy was the leading representative and the other reps—men like Oscar Robertson, Cincinnati, Bob Pettit, St. Louis, Jerry West, Los Angeles—wanted to know what the next move would be.

The delaying tactics continued as we headed into the final thirty minutes before television time. We called a meeting in the Eastern All Stars dressing room. The Western squad came down.

It was put to the group that they were the strongest representation of the NBA, its major stars, and that unless we took a stand then and there the owners would never heed the desires of the players again.

We took a strike vote. The first time it was eleven to nine against the strike.

So, democratically, we voted again. This time it was eleven to nine in favor.

Silence, vast nervous silence descended on the room as Heinsohn went out to deliver his ultimatum. Fifteen minutes remained before the game. One super star started to stutter. "W-w-w-ell, we h-h-h-ave to-to understand t-t-their p-p-point," said this giant who usually had perfect diction.

"Shut up," someone said.

Another super star sat there in a crouch, his hands shaking so badly he had to sit on them.

Heinsohn returned. Ten minutes to game time. No answer. Los Angeles owner Bob Short stormed into the adjacent trainer's room. We could hear—as he knew—his threats.

"If any of my players are in on this, then they're through. Finished for life. They're blowing a hundred grand between them."

Jerry West looked at Elgin Baylor. They sat quietly and waited. The threats went on.

Five minutes. The door opened. It was J. Walter Kennedy. The owners—unable to agree even to meet until confronted with this ultimatum—had held a quick meeting in a back room. They would talk to us about pensions at the May meeting.

We played. Their national television deal wasn't spoiled. In May, they finally did begin negotiations on some of our considerations, but we received little other than a token pension plan, a modest amount whereby we contribute $500 of our salaries. The fight for other concessions—fewer exhibition games, carrying trainers and so forth—is still going on. It will probably continue forever. It is one of the facts of the league and one of the things that keeps it from being great.

Take the matter of trainers. For eight years, the Celtics have had LeRoux, who does many extra things in addition to training. But as a trainer alone he has saved many a player from serious injury.

As a matter of practical business, it makes sense to have a trainer with the team. A slightly injured player, without proper treatment, can sustain a serious, career-crippling injury. The loss can mean a championship, as witness Elgin Baylor's knee injury.

The owners refuse to buy it. They say the cost of trainer, including transportation, would amount to over $30,000 a year. We've argued back, "Then carry one less player, but use the trainer." With an eye on expansion, they won't buy that either.

I don't know how I got mixed up in all this bit of unionism, but it sounded like the right thing to me, so I participated. Ironically, only high-ranking ball players were involved in the threatened strike— All Stars, men making over $25,000 a year.

We were fighting for the little guy who comes into the league and gets $7500 to start and may never work his way up to more than $14,000 after five good years. We wanted to give them some security. For that reason alone, I think it was laudable. Here was a clear case of twenty big stars looking out for their teammates, albeit some of the big stars were afflicted with strong feelings akin to being a chicken when the pressure built up.

Heinsohn came out of it worst of all. Brown, great as he was, had an explosive temper and he felt that this strike was an embarrassment to him since it was led by his own players and was staged in his own Boston Garden.

"In my opinion, Tommy Heinsohn is the greatest heel in the history of sports," he said.

The story became a big one all over the country and while it did not greatly hamper the play of the Celtics it was an underlying factor as we started the march towards our seventh world championship.

Auerbach finally put Brown and Heinsohn together in a meeting which looked like a small summit conference.

They met for half an hour and Heinsohn—who was ready to quit—told Brown his side. Brown stuck to his guns. "I'll go along with the need for a pension plan," he said, "but I won't change my mind about Heinsohn. He's still a heel."

Poor Tommy had to stand there and take it. Brown

never did talk to him again until the end of the year when he finally came in and shook his hand.

As you can see, a certain amount of delicate balance is required to keep a world championship team running under all these conditions. Another secret of the Celtics is that we were always able to sublimate outside pressures and get along as a group ourselves.

Much of this credit should go to Auerbach. In my opinion, the man is the genius of sports. He is not always right. He is an egotist who has a terrible temper and he is a man who can go off the deep end sometimes. He can be as gruff and as nasty and miserable a human being as you want to meet. Conversely, he can be quiet, peaceful and a decent guy.

Either way, he is a man who at the age of forty-nine has worked his way up from the pavement of the Williamsburg section of Brooklyn to become the leading coach in the world today and darn close to being a millionaire. That road isn't easy to follow and credit is due to Auerbach for having achieved it.

Among his accomplishments was assembling the rest of the cast of characters who went on to make the Celtics great.

Cousy, Sharman, Ramsey, Heinsohn, Risen, Loscutoff, Phillip were the nucleus from which he started.

Then, as the years went on, he picked up—in this order—Sam Jones (North Carolina), K.C. Jones (when he got out of the Army), Tom Sanders (NYU), John Havlicek (Ohio State), Larry Siegfried (Ohio State), Willie Naulls (UCLA) and an assortment of persons who were just passing through. This includes old pros such as Clyde Lovellette, who was with us two years (1962-63), Dan Swartz, who came out of the other league which folded (American Conference), baseball pitcher Gene Conley, and our new rookies, John Thompson, Ron Bonham and Mel Counts.

Sam Jones was the first to join us, coming aboard in the fall of 1957. Auerbach called me in San Francisco— and this is a fine-line thing, but it's one of those issues which can burn you a little.

"How about Sam Jones? Do you think he can go good for us?" Auerbach asked.

"Who the hell is Sam Jones?" I asked.

"He's a Schvartzer [Ed.—Yiddish for Black] who plays for North Carolina," Auerbach said. "I thought you'd know about him."

"Look, Red," I said, "I really don't know all of them."

It burned me because this is a form of—what shall we call it—looking down your nose? Maybe. I dunno. I mean, is Auerbach supposed to know every player in the world who is Jewish just because he's Jewish?

This is an innocent approach. But it is a form of prejudice, a form of pigeonholing. All Negroes are supposed to know all other Negroes. Why?

Two quick examples of the way an unthinking non-black can bother a Negro without intent. I'm sitting in the locker-room getting ready for a game and Red brings in a man from a major international firm with which I have dealings on my plantation. It happens that I know the president of the company, many of the vice-presidents. But the man, trying to make conversation, asks me only: "Do you know Charlie Smith?" Now who is Charlie Smith? It turns out I should only know him because he is also a Negro.

Or this one, much more funny. It happened as I was writing this book. We were on an exhibition trip in San Francisco and an old high school teammate of mine, Bob Hodges, was joining me for lunch. We went into the parking lot and he had to pull his car out. I was standing there all dressed up and a lady drove in and said: "Where should I park this?"

Automatically, I was the attendant.

I said: "Oh, put it over there," and she began backing and hauling and pulling her car into a space and the attendant came over and said: "Get that car out of there."

She said: "But he told me to put it there."

I smiled and said: "That's right. But I don't care where you put it, lady. I don't work here."

A small, humorous victory.

Know him or not, though, there was no doubt that Sam Jones was going to be a big league basketball player. He came to live with Rose and me that first season and through the years he grew from a sub backcourt-man into a starter and into a super star.

Sam always has played under a different philosophy than some of us. Sam figured the thing to do was to always keep something in reserve for next year.

Each season he adds to his average and comes up with an extra shot every other year. I think this time (1965) he's using a two-hander with higher loft that he has been saving since he was a freshman in college.

Sam was never kidding us, though. We knew all along that he was pacing himself. You run into this a lot in all professional sports. Like a certain baseball player who won fifteen games one year, seventeen the next, and then nineteen. I was talking with him and I said, "One more and you'll have twenty wins."

"Gee," he said, "I don't want to spoil them. I'd rather wait until another year and not wreck my arm and they'll have to keep raising my salary every season. If I win twenty now they'll expect me to always win twenty."

Sam Jones played the same way. What he didn't realize was that he could have been making more money earlier had he gone all out. But then, Sam will be playing another seven years and maybe his idea is right for him.

One thing you can say for Sam is that he really has the shot. When he throws that one-banker, it really goes in beautifully. And under pressure he is one of the greatest clutch players of the Celtics.

You might be surprised at the number of shooters who suddenly get a case of the "don't give it to me's" under real pressure. All season long they run with their heads up, looking, pleading, yelling for the ball. They love what we call "garbage-up time," making points that have no real effect on the outcome. Watch some of them in the last minute of the playoffs, though. They have their heads down. I think they're praying: "Oh, not me. Please don't make me shoot. I might be the goat." That was never the case with Sam.

Give me the man everytime who'll throw it up and Katie-bar-the-door. That's a pro.

Sam, Cooz, Heinsohn, all the rest proved themselves to be champions and there is a marked difference between being a champion and being merely great.

Perhaps it is just the élan of playing under pressure. Through my mind flits the vignette of a key playoff game with Philadelphia: Chamberlain standing there in the final minute guarding the basket, all seven feet of him looking like the end of the world and the Celtics trailing by a point and the clock about to go off and Cousy comes charging down at Wilt and goes right up over him and lays one in.

For all the marbles. For all the knockers who would have asked for a hundred years: "What happened?" if he had missed.

As a champion, he didn't miss.

Or Sam Jones, restless, moving, upset, determined, showing up at the Garden one afternoon before our seventh game with Cincinnati in 1963. Sam Jones practicing in the darkness of the Garden all alone, all afternoon long. Then Sam went out and scored forty-seven points.

A champion.

All champions must be that way. It is the rule of holding the title, from the smallest championship of a junior high school to the biggest. A champion must forget greatness and must be simply the man that you have to beat at his best under pressure. Few men ever get the chance to find out.

We did.

They—the Celtics—were all champions.


K.C. Jones came aboard in the fall of 1959. He had been in the Army and when he came out he tried out for the Los Angeles Rams as a halfback. We had never had a football team at USF, but K.C. was so great that even so he made the club.

Not a bad stunt.

Auerbach was on him to play pro basketball, though, and K.C. decided to pack in football and go along with basketball.

It led to a bad thing. Someone wrote that K.C. Jones would never make the Celtics except as a friend of Bill Russell's and only because Russell demanded it.

We were out of town when the story ran. It really hurt K.C. and it damned near ruined him before he even got started in pro sports. He was really upset. I went storming into Auerbach and I put it right on him:

"Is that right? Does K.C. Jones play only because of me, because if that's a fact then you can forget it."

Auerbach put his feet on the desk and blew a smoke ring with his cigar and said:

"Listen. My own brother wouldn't play on this team if he couldn't cut it. Dumb sportswriters I can't help. You got real problems, come and see me."

K.C. Jones stayed on his own merit and as the years went on became noted as the greatest defensive backcourtman in the game. He had one problem—he was afraid to shoot.

Auerback demanded more and more that K.C. take a shot and take charge. We could have told him that K.C. could take charge all right. At USF he had many of the same plays Cousy made famous; the behind-the-back pass, the long set shot (which K.C. fired from the hip), and that great defense which has since made him a superb star. More than that, K.C. has the most fantastic basketball mind I have ever seen. He can make up whole patterns in a split second, can grasp the issue quicker and command a situation more certainly than any man I have ever seen. His one problem was that he was following Cousy and he didn't want to appear to be copying him. A man must have his pride. We had to work on it, forcing him more and more into the role which was naturally his. No one accepts a challenge more than the handsome man with the square eyes. He took up the slack and then some.

He ran into only one disaster and that came as the 1965 exhibition season began. K.C. had worn a brace on his front uppers for a year to straighten out his two center teeth. It was painful, but he put up with it. Now, we were leaving for the exhibition series and the teeth were nearly perfect, really beautiful. In Missoula, Montana, on our third exhibition game with the Los Angeles Lakers someone stuck out an elbow and K.C. lost his two front teeth. All for $10 a day eating money, which is all we get paid in the exhibition season. Oh well, he had to come up a loser sometimes.

The arrival of two additional Negroes added a little

more fuel to the flaming issue of segregation in basketball. In 1958 I had said very frankly that there was a quota. This had been denied, but the quota was still in effect, although the game was changing drastically and more and more Negroes were being acknowledged as stars.

Now, in this same year, we also had a fourth Negro player, our number one draft choice, Ben Swain of Texas State.

A sportswriter finally crystallized exactly what I had been talking about when he wrote: "The Celtics will not keep four Negroes. The crowds won't stand for it and neither will the owners."

He was not intending to help the Negro cause in his story, but he unintentionally did because I seized on it to confront Brown and Auerbach with the issue again.

"Now, tell me."

They told me. "Just like before," said Brown, who had brought in the first Negro in the NBA (Chuck Cooper). "I look for players, black, white, vermilion, I couldn't care less."

Auerbach agreed with him. Now, it is about equal four or five Negroes on each team in the NBA and no one thinks much of it any more. But in those days it was a big thing.

Brown could never believe that there was a quota. Once, at an All Star Game luncheon in Boston, a *Saturday Evening Post* story I had written stated there was a quota and Brown got up and said there wasn't.

I didn't say a word for the press. Afterwards, I took him aside and said: "Mr. Brown, I have too much respect for you to ever argue with you in public. But there is a quota. And I have purposely gone out on a limb about it because I figure it will take the heat off the owners. All the fans will be too busy hating me and too busy trying to prove there isn't a quota to pay any attention while you owners do away with it."

I think it worked out just that way. I don't want any misunderstanding here. I am not taking the credit for it. But I was trying to do my share.

It wasn't something the Negro manufactured. We

knew darn well that we were on the spot. But we knew that it was a complete injustice, that there wasn't a single reason why this kind of latent anti-black prejudice should interfere with a basic American sport. The years, in a sense—and the fans, in a definite sense—proved us right. It didn't hurt the attendance. It didn't hurt the game.

One of the nicer human beings who joined us next was Tom Sanders, a very erudite, soft-spoken All-American from NYU. Sanders was the biggest, gawkiest, funniest looking thing we had ever seen. He wore glasses with a big thong around them to hold them in place and he had knee pads. The Celtics got him contact lenses, but they couldn't do anything about the pads. Then, on the first day of practice, Auerbach and Ramsey clipped the pads. Sanders looked high and low for them. "Red, I can't go on," he said. "I don't have my pads."

The rest of us were breaking up with laughter.

"Listen," Auerbach said, "you got a broken elbow? You got a broken knee?"

"No," said Sanders, "but I never played without my pads."

"Well, you're playing without them now, baby," Auerbach said. "Get out there."

Sanders has never worn pads since. His contact lenses have always plagued us, though. They're always falling out. Once in a game we were all—both sides—on our hands and knees crawling around on the court looking for his lens.

I finally found it. "Here, 'Satch.' Do I have to do everything on this team?"

"Satch" has always been one of our best-loved figures and one whom we like to talk about (maybe it is because he doesn't talk back).

His two classics were as follows:

In the winter of the 1962-63 season we were playing Baltimore and LeRoux was friendly with Jack McNally of the White House staff. The Celtics were staying in Washington and McNally invited them over to the

White House. Unfortunately, I didn't get the word, so I wasn't present.

When the President heard that the Celtics were in the building he asked them to drop by the office. For about fifteen minutes they waited in the Cabinet Room (oh, how Auerbach must have loved sitting there). Then they were brought in to see President Kennedy and spent about half an hour chatting with him.

Now, they were on their way out the door, each man stopping to shake hands with the President and say a few words. Satch was last in the line and he is so shy that he was naturally nervous.

He was searching for something to say. Finally, the moment approached and he shook hands and, searching desperately, said: "Take it easy, baby."

The President broke up. So did the Celtics. It became a slogan for a long time. And, I am told, it also became an oft-used phrase around the Oval Room. JFK had much going for him. Including a remarkable sense of humor.

Then there was the day Sanders got his first automobile license at the Boston Registry.

He was extra proud of it. His first car. His first license. He left the Registry pleased as punch and he was passing in front of it when a truck started nosing into the intersection. A policeman stood in front with his arm raised to halt traffic for pedestrians, but Satch was only watching the truck and he kept right on crawling at five miles an hour and he just nudged the cop.

Satch stopped with a very innocent "Who me, officer?" look on his face.

The cop said: "Let me see your license."

Pleased as punch, Satch produced it.

It was exactly fifteen minutes old.

The cop just said: "Oh, get outta here."


The last major figure in the cast was a block-shouldered, hard-nosed kid named Johnny Havlicek. We call him "Spider." His hands are everywhere.

Havlicek was the forgotten man of the Ohio State team which starred Jerry Lucas. (Larry Siegfried, also a Celtic, was the Captain of the same squad).

Havlicek was a forward, but Lucas was the shooter

and as an All-American was the natural territorial draft choice of the Cincinnati Royals. They fully expected that they could pick Havlicek up the next time around. Auerbach swooped in and grabbed him.

It was a practical demonstration of an Auerbach theory at work—given a choice, always pick a college player who is used to playing on a winner.

He picked a beauty in Havlicek. He probably has more desire and more courage than anyone who ever came out of Ohio State.

On the Celtics, he has been forced to make the difficult adjustment into the role of sixth man, replacing Ramsey. The role fits him beautifully.

Havlicek has one habit which I think is incorrect—he dribbles with his head down. If he ever learns to keep his head up, he will be a super star. If he doesn't, he will still always rate on my all time Celtics team.

Havlicek and Siegfried (we call the latter "Flakey," but it is a term of endearment, because we love him) have provided us with some great moments, not the least of which stem from their status as bachelors.

In 1964, we flew to Cincinnati for a key game. Heavy winds blew up around Cleveland and we were forced to land. We rented a bus to make the ride to Cinci and Havlicek and Siegfried argued with the driver for half an hour about the logical shortcuts to Cincinnati. They finally convinced him it was through some town off the beaten path. So we did it. Then they had a place which would be great for us to stop for dinner. So we stopped. They both made a beeline for the phone booth. The only reason for the shortcut and the stop, it turned out, was that they each had a girl-friend in the town.

Characters.

So were they all. The old professionals who were playing out the string with us; the super stars who made us champions; the determined, dogged fighters who gave us the juice to keep going; the young rookies who came in and proved they had a place on the squad.

The biggest character of all was the balding little man with the big bank account.

Arnold Auerbach.

The dictator.

The man who ran this team like a symphony, covering all the discordant notes beneath the sheer momentum of the score.

Auerbach . . . the real character of our cast.

# CHAPTER V

## AUERBACH AND ME

The name is Red. It doesn't fit much any more. He is practically bald and every hair in his head is gray.

Still, if you were to rate the greatest coaches in the history of sports, his name must top the list.

Given a choice, I would play for no other man in the world.

Yet, we are not particularly friends. No man who has played for Auerbach has ever been close to him, with the possible exception of Cousy.

I do not know what Auerbach's politics are, but he certainly cannot be described as a liberal as a coach. His philosophy is expressed best by himself:

"Cry me no tears. Tell me no sad tales. This team is a totalitarian state and I alone am the dictator."

He means it. No man crosses Auerbach and remains with the Celtics. It can be anything Auerbach decides is a cross-up—not staying in shape, not catching a plane, leading a rookie astray.

His secrets? They are many. He knows exactly the right way to select a player—rookie or old pro—and move him onto a squad without disrupting the fluidity of the team. A tough kid who fought his way up from the streets of Brooklyn, he never deludes himself.

Auerbach has a reason for everything, from yelling at a referee to selling out the Garden with a promotion to bringing in a player who, on the surface, appears to be useless.

Auerbach cannot stand the thought of losing. Neither can I. Anyone who has ever come to the Celtics has been immediately instilled with this philosophy. If you don't play to win, Auerbach has no place for you.

He has pulled off some fantastic deals. He brought Gene Conley back to basketball from baseball and used him for two years because he computed that Conley could play ten minutes a game and supply the extra muscle which might be needed in a tight spot. Conley could jump higher than anyone in the league. Red figured that every time Gene could get the ball he was accounting for four points—two for us and two the other side didn't get.

When Conley left, he picked up Clyde Lovellette from St. Louis. Then he brought Willie Naulls back when he left the Knicks.

Auerbach put Willie on the team fully knowing that he had a weight problem which no one else would touch. Working carefully with our trainer, he changed Willie's whole life, trimming him down from a 245-pound whale to a handsome, svelte 190-pound forward.

When we talk about Willie now we never mention the whale part. We call him "Sweetcakes" because he is so pretty.

Willie has a terrible time getting into shape for the season because he has a basically weak constitution. But he has the heart of a lion.

Auerbach long ago developed the theory that if he could drive his team into top physical shape before the season started, he would have an edge on the rest of the league. On most teams, the stars play themselves into shape.

Not so with Auerbach. He starts off with the toughest possible two-a-day training schedule and no one is exempted. For one solid month, it's run-run-run and by the time the season opens the Celtics usually spring right out of the box and run away from everyone. That explains the secret behind our winning streaks when we opened the year up and just kept on rolling.

In Willie's case, though, we knew every year that at the start of training Auerbach was going to run Willie right into a state of unconsciousness. I've seen Willie fall down bleeding from the nose. Fainted. Completely out of it. But up he'd get again and start playing and off he'd go and this is one reason why he stuck with the Celtics. Auerbach loves a display of guts.

This technique of getting into shape, coupled with the work of our trainer, results in fewer injuries to the starters.

LeRoux, an ex-hockey trainer who was borrowed from the Bruins for one game back in 1959, is a master at the art of taping and treating injuries as well as practicing preventive medicine.

The LeRoux story is typical of how Arnold Auerbach runs the show. Our old trainer, the late Harvey Cohn, was ill in 1959 and Auerbach asked the Bruins' coach, Milt Schmidt, if he could borrow his assistant trainer, LeRoux. Schmidt, coming up to the playoffs, agreed for one game, but pointed out he had to have Buddy back before the playoffs.

Red said "Sure." He liked the way Buddy worked, however, and every day Schmidt would come to the door of the office and attempt to get Buddy back and Auerbach would say: "What agreement? What deal? He stays with me."

LeRoux has been with him ever since.

In the main, Auerbach does his own scouting, with occasional help from old players like Bones McKinney (he found Sam Jones) and Ramsey and Bob Brannum.

This has led to a remarkable streak. Auerbach is seldom far off on a player. The only year he was really off was when we picked Bill Green as our number one draft choice in 1963.

Green was a good ballplayer. The only thing was that Auerbach never thought to ask him if he minded flying. We were taking off on the first exhibition of the season—skipping back and forth across the country—and Green came to Auerbach and asked if he could have his bus ticket.

"Bus ticket? What the hell has a bus ticket got to do with this?" Auerbach screamed.

"Oh. I never fly," said Green.

That was our number one draft choice, carefully culled

by Auerbach over a long, tough season. Green didn't make the team. I think we lost him when he missed a bus connection between Owensboro, Ky., and Kansas City.

Auerbach now has that vital question on his check list.

Of course, some of the planes Auerbach picks make you think Green might have been right.

Auerbach is famous for some classics. He believes in getting his team up early in the morning (like 6 A.M. after a game which ended at midnight) and flying on to the next town. The theory works. Would that the planes worked as well.

Conscious of this, Auerbach decided to make it all up to us in 1963 when we were involved in the tough series with Cincinnati. We had a chartered C-47 waiting for us immediately after the second game in Boston.

It was a plush executive job with easy chairs and tables and so forth.

Very comfortable to fly in.

Except that we flew.

And flew.

And flew.

It is four hours to Cinci commercially, right? Counting time in airports.

Well, after four hours we were landing at Buffalo. Why Buffalo? Simple. It was the only airport where the pilot's gas credit card was good. The world champions munched candy bars at the closed airport and then we trundled on towards Cincinnati. We arrived at 7 A.M. We received quite a welcome. We could hear the airport transmitting as we started down: "You're off the glide path . . . you're too high on the glide path . . . YOU'RE TOO HIGH ON THE GLIDE PATH . . ."

At the time, I was losing in the poker game and I said: "It might as well crash. It's the only way I can get even."

The pilot finally found the glide path after much struggling (maybe he wasn't used to flying in dawn's early light) and we landed, took the long ride into Cinci, collapsed in the hotel and then proceeded to get murdered in the game that night.

That was the end of Arnold's generosity to us with special charters.

I won't bore you with some of the other planes we've taken. But, if there is any way to get into trouble with a plane that we haven't had, then it doesn't exist. Arnold can pick them all right.

We always remind him that we're champions and shudder to think what we might have to fly if we ever come up losers. The Red Sox, for example, were the subject of one of the funniest remarks of all time—airborne, that is—when they were coming home after losing umpty-ump straight. They were flying through a thunderstorm. The plane was pitching and rocking and Frank Sullivan, a pitcher of that era and the team tummeler, looked out at a particularly close burst of lightning and said:

"This team is insured for two million dollars. Sort of makes you wonder which way the front office is rooting, doesn't it?"

All I can say is, if you want to play pro sports, bring your dramamine and be prepared. If you don't fly, you don't play.

About as witty was the remark of Syracuse's Johnny Kerr one night in 1962. Syracuse, Philadelphia and Boston were all on the same plane, flying from one doubleheader to another and locked in a fairly tight race for the division title. New York was seventeen games off our pace.

The plane started going through those tantrums that planes do and Kerr said in the stillness of our sheer panic:

"Well, I guess New York is in first place."

A funny man.

One time, Auerbach outthought himself.

It was in 1960 when we tied the record for most consecutive victories. We had won seventeen straight and were playing Cincinnati in Detroit. It was New Year's Eve.

Auerbach figured he would keep the whole gang together. No chance of big heads when we went for the record.

"We'll have our own private party in my suite," he said. "Ginger-ale, potato-chips, Cokes. Then at 1 A.M. we'll all be in bed."

We were. There were no more sober citizens in the

United States on New Year's Eve than the Celtics that night in Detroit.

The next evening, January 1, we went to the Olympiad to play Cincinnati, which was a very weak team at that time.

They killed us.

Auerbach has never thrown a New Year's party since.

But we've spent a lot of lonely ones. I mean, have you ever been in Syracuse on New Year's Eve—with a lousy movie on the late show?

If one were to develop Auerbach's theory on coaching in full, it could be summed up in a brass-bound book, the cover of which would be inscribed:

### SCREAM
### By Red Auerbach

I was playing with the word CHEAT, but that's not Red's style, although his philosophy is to get everything he can by fair means and more diverse methods.

Auerbach is the past master of the psychology of the game. Both of the game of sports and of life.

To sum him up very precisely, I would say this:

As a man and as a coach, Auerbach never does anything without a reason. I have never seen him have an accident of any kind in his dealings with individuals, in business or in the world of sports.

He has come a long way and it has been a hard one. But do not be deluded into thinking that the Celtics have all been Arnold Auerbach's genius as a coach, and know full well that among professionals a super star must make himself. It is not the coaching which makes a Baylor or a Pettit or a Cousy or a Chamberlain.

Auerbach has always been aware of this vast differentiation.

He long since put his finger on the major difference between being a professional coach and a college or high school coach.

In the pros, a coach is responsible not to the players, but to the team. He must find the best man and utilize him.

One great misnomer about pro sports is the theory of the team leader. Among professionals I do not believe there is anything like a team leader. The play of a professional cannot be improved by association with a leader type. Nor can a professional be inspired to play better than he is just because he is emotionally stimulated by watching a teammate play better.

Professional athletics is like any other profession—just that. A profession. You always do the best you can. Auerbach realizes this.

There are times when I have personally thought that he made mistakes, but I will give him the benefit of the doubt and say that he is human, too.

There are some in the NBA who won't go that far.

It would be pleasant if in describing our coach-general-manager-rich man I said that throughout the Celtics there has always been a distinctive, hail-fellow-well-met, gee-he's-one-of-my-team spirit about the man in charge.

It would also be a lie.

Rather, I would describe the relationship as cordial, but not deep.

Auerbach believes that he should not associate with his players—or with their wives.

Thus, he is, in fact, a lonely man, a man who spends the lonely months of the season locked up in his hotel room, eating Chinese food off a hot plate, or, when we are on the road, spending most of his time with LeRoux.

The only player he was ever close to was Bob Cousy and this was the result of a friendship which sprang up in 1954 on an overseas trip to Africa.

Frankly, I did not fare so well on my last overseas trip with Auerbach. We were all together on a team which made the first trip behind the Iron Curtain.

In six weeks, we made the grand tour—Yugoslavia, Rumania, United Arab Republic, Poland.

An amateur team had gone overseas earlier that year and they were savaged by the opposition, including some disastrous losses to the Russian team which was getting ready for the Olympics in Japan.

I would point out here that there is a vast difference between our amateurs and those of the nations behind the Iron Curtain. The Yugoslavians and the Russians devote years to training their athletes, who, in effect, might be considered professionals. Since they do not have professional leagues, the Iron Curtain fans assumed that our amateurs were an equal for their version of amateurs and the United States was dealt a tremendous loss of face by the disastrous trip. (Nineteen losses.)

Enter the professional basketball players.

Auerbach had experience guiding trips before. For one thing, he has an idea in the back of his mind that there should be an Under Secretary of State for Athletic Affairs and that a well-manned, well-directed office of this type would do much to correct the overseas image of the United States in both the Olympics and in the regular annual games between nations.

I would not say that he personally seeks the office, but he has talked so much about it that I think it probable he would not exactly turn it down.

As a matter of fact, I would endorse him for it. If I know Arnold, he would not come up a loser, personally, or in his involvement with teams.

On this particular trip, we played twenty-one games and won them all. We were supposed to play the Russians, but they declined and we never did get there.

The team was composed of Bob Cousy, Tom Gola of San Francisco, Bob Pettit of St. Louis, Oscar Robertson and Jerry Lucas of Cincinnati, K.C. and Heinsohn, plus Auerbach, LeRoux and myself.

We had just won our seventh world championship by beating San Francisco in April and now, early May, we shook hands with L.B.J. and departed. Lest one think that we were motivated by sheer patriotism, let me point out that anyone who makes this kind of trip gets paid for it.

In my case, I got $200 a week. It's not such a big deal as you might think. I earn about $2000 a week, so there is some loss. Still, since I am telling truths here, don't make the mistake of thinking that we all go on the arm, for zero. Pros aren't made that way.

The trip took us to Poland first and it was here that Cousy and Auerbach pulled their gag on Heinsohn.

The Hawk is of German descent and he looks it and, of course, the Poles are not exactly deeply enthralled with things or people German.

Everywhere we went, Cousy and Auerbach would make a point of saying about Heinsohn: "German . . . Hun . . ." and pointing. When they called him by his nickname of "Heinie" everyone turned to stare.

It had Heinsohn off his feed. One night in Warsaw, Heinsohn was sitting in his room with Gola and Lucas. Gola was shaving. Two guys in trenchcoats walked in. One showed a badge of some sort and said to Heinsohn: "You. Come with us."

Heinsohn was in a state of shock. Gola kept right on shaving and Lucas kept right on reading his book. The funny thing is that they thought it was for real.

A knee-shaking, pale Heinsohn was led away, down the stairs and through the lobby. It happened that Cousy, Auerbach and LeRoux were hiding in the hall, choking on their laughter.

LeRoux sped down to the room and there was Gola shaving and Lucas reading his book and LeRoux asked where Heinsohn was.

Without missing a stroke, Gola said: "Oh, they just arrested him."

He must have been mentally counting the winning share of the next year's playoffs.

Now, the guys in the trenchcoats took Heinsohn into a restaurant and said: "You wait."

They were supposed to take him to the lobby of a police station and leave him there, but that's kind of carrying a gag too far behind the Iron Curtain.

The Hawk was sitting there, smoking three and four cigarettes at a time, when Auerbach and Cousy came in. He was all alone and really shocked. Then they let him in on the gag. The two chaps in trenchcoats were Polish basketball coaches.

Some Bulgarian students were in Poland and they asked to see me. They were immediately in sympathy with the cause of the American Negro and were asking me all kinds of questions, to which I was replying as truthfully as I could, at the same time fully understanding that their statements about it never happening in Bulgaria were true only because there were probably only two Negroes in the whole country.

Finally, after long protests about how they, as humanitarians, fully understood the American Negro and his problems, one of their spokesmen said: "And now, would you please sing us a song or do a dance. How about 'Go Down Moses'?"

I broke up. To me, it was even funnier than the Heinsohn incident. But then maybe I have a warped sense of humor about the plight of the American Negro as viewed through the eyes of the "liberal" Bulgarians.

Not so funny on our trip were our visits to concentration camps like Auschwitz. A man who believes in saying what he thinks, popular or not, can learn a lesson about the value of standing up for a cause from what happened there.

Also not so funny, in my opinion, was the attitude of Auerbach, which transcended the norm. Perhaps he was working too hard.

There were several incidents among our player personnel. Finally, it came to a head in Yugoslavia.

I have a laugh which I suppose can be grating. But it's mine. I've been using it for years. When I laugh, I laugh. It was nothing new to Auerbach. But someone said something funny and Auerbach started yelling: "Russell, you be quiet."

I said it succinctly and to the point:

"— —, Red. Don't say anything to me. Not ever."

It marked a first in my career. And a last. But no man worth his salt takes a pushing around forever.

Hence, one might say my personal relationship with Auerbach can only be considered cordial.

Throughout this, I must continue to add that I respect Auerbach as a professional coach, fully acknowledging now that we are talking in terms of professional sports, not those of the happy amateur.

# CHAPTER VI

## "IT"

As far as Auerbach's attitude towards Negroes, I feel in all honesty that he can be characterized as a middle-of-the-roader.

There were a couple of problems which arose in games in segregated towns. In 1958 we had a regular season game scheduled in Charlotte, North Carolina. I asked Red about it.

"No sweat," he said. "We played there with Chuck Cooper."

I took him at his word. I didn't know that when Chuck Cooper played there he was segregated and left town on the late sleeper. Cousy accompaneid him as a matter of pure-hearted gentlemanly protest.

When we were flying down to Charlotte, Red wasn't with us. LeRoux said to Sam Jones and me—he was embarrassed, but the fall guy—"You fellows will be staying at the so-and-so hotel."

I said: "Wait a minute. What's this you fellows stuff?"

It didn't matter. We were staying at the so-and-so hotel and you could really call it so-and-so all right. There were roaches everywhere. A real dump.

Being professionals, we had to play the game. For some strange reason, Arnold was absent until late in the day.

When he arrived, I telephoned him and the rest of the team at their—at least by comparison—palatial hotel.

"Oh, it isn't that bad," Auerbach said.

"It is to me, Red. I blame you for bringing this team here," I said.

"Look, I have to be careful. Remember, I'm Jewish," Auerbach answered.

To which I replied: "Oh yeah? Well, what hotel are you staying in, Red?"

That was the end of it, but it left a real bad feeling in our hearts. I submit to any reader that it would. A man is a man is a man. A team is a team is a team, with apologies to Gertrude Stein and with the heart-felt hope that the explanation will show why the American Negro, athlete, super star, hard worker, man or whatever, has feelings like anyone else.

After the game, some sportswriter remarked to me about the fact that the Celtics seem to have fun. This might be true. We bore no permanent grudge against our teammates and in the locker-room we laughed with the rest of the team. But when he asked I told him: "Well, I'll tell you the unfunniest thing that ever happened to me. That was playing in this crummy town. I'll never play here again."

It made the wire services and Auerbach later said: "Russell can't speak for the entire team."

This is true. I was speaking for Russell . . . man, Negro, basketball player, American citizen.

A month later, Elgin Baylor ran into a similar situation in West Virginia. The Lakers played without him.

There were several other incidents and, mark you, I use these not as an indictment of Red Auerbach or the Boston Celtics or the United States. But a fact is a fact and since we are telling the story of an American who also happens to be a Negro—and proud and pleased to be one—I feel that the story should be told. Only through candor does understanding come about.

Another place "it" happened was in Marion, Indiana. The team arrived and the Mayor gave us the keys to the city. Much later that night, K.C. Jones, Carl Braun (white) and I went to a restaurant to eat.

The manager said all the tables were reserved. The place was empty, but we said we would stand at the bar. "That's reserved, too," the manager said.

I went to police headquarters to file a complaint. Nobody would take it. There was one Negro police officer in the back room—isn't that always the way?—and the desk sergeant asked us to talk to him. We did. He explained: "These are nice people. Don't rock the boat."

Not for me, baby. I fight things that I think are wrong. We asked to see the Mayor, but, strangely, no one could remember where he lived. We finally found out and the next morning we swore out a complaint, the Mayor agreeing that the actions of the restaurant were against the law.

The manager denied it. But we signed the complaint and K.C. Jones, who never gets mad, told him: "You're a liar."

K.C. told him right.

It was a matter of men doing what they thought was right. Simply that. I ask you—how can you get the key to a city in the morning and be told to go hungry in the evening?

There was one other major incident during my years with the Celtics. There were two really. One came during a non-Celtic NBA All Star exhibition tour after the 1958 playoffs. We were being paid in good, cold cash per game so don't think that I only do this when I'm already on a seasonal payroll.

Dallas was on the schedule and we were told Negro members of the team would be treated as much like Americans as anyone else.

We flew from Louisville to Dallas in a DC-3 on a particularly bad day. The plane almost crashed. We were late getting in. When we arrived, the promoter still said everything was all right, although I wanted to call the hotel from the airport. But we went and played because we were late.

When we finally got to the hotel, the promoter and his local aide said: 'You're going to stay at. . . ."

No thanks, baby. Money never meant that much to me.

They protested it wasn't their fault. The man put out his hand for me to shake. I spat at it. I went back to the airport and flew home. It cost me several thousand dollars. About one quarter of what I was earning that year. I was broke. But I was a man. I would do it again. It is the people who say they're not responsible who are just as responsible as anyone else.

The only thing you can do is make the cost of being a bigot just that—costly. I try. It cost them on the tour.

Regrettably, it cost me, too. But it was worth it. Success in having all Americans just that—all Americans—will only come when the cost of being a bigot becomes too high to pay.

Another time, I was going to Miami for an exhibition. They told me the hotel was all right. I called up and the guy said: "Yes."

I didn't believe it. I stayed on him. Finally, he said, "Oh yes. You can stay here. You may use the dining room and the swimming pool. We ask only one thing. Be inconspicuous."

I broke up in laughter and in anger.

Six-10. A Negro. Wearing a beard. Can you just see me using the swimming pool and being inconspicuous?

I checked into a Negro hotel, instead. It wasn't like the one in North Carolina. I had a ball.

And got a suntan.

The other time "it" happened with the Celtics was in Lexington, Kentucky.

Ramsey was an All-American graduate of the University of Kentucky and it was a Homecoming Day Exhibition with St. Louis for Rams and his Kentucky teammate (then with the Hawks) Cliff Hagan.

We flew all day from Wichita to Lexington and had no breakfast or lunch. We checked into the hotel.

I was just leaving my room to eat when Sam Jones and Tom Sanders came down the hall and met K.C. and me.

"Where are you going?" they asked.

"To get something to eat in the coffee-shop," K.C. said.

"Not down there you're not," said Sam.

They had gone in to eat and the waitress refused to serve them.

I just went back in the room and called the airport. "I would like a plane," I said.

"To where?" asked the girl.

"Whichever is the next plane going to Washington, New York or Chicago," I said.

I told "you guys" that I was leaving. They could guide themselves accordingly.

They all wanted to leave.

Al Butler, another teammate, was absent from the hotel and we couldn't find him. We did see Woody Sauldsberry and Cleo Hill of St. Louis and informed them of the circumstances of our "residence" in this palatial hostelry for Americans and they left as well.

Next, we called Auerbach who tried to convince us that it was better for our race, better for all Negroes, if we stayed. I was sick and tired of that argument. I believe, most sincerely, that for decades a proud race—the American Negro—has attempted to make it better "for your people" by playing the game of life with bigots by maintaining the status quo. It never worked. The only way to gain rights is to fight for them. Regardless of whether I was suspended, fined, or whatever, I was going to fight.

"I speak for no one but myself, Red," I said. "I'm leaving. I've gone through all the arguments. I am simply no longer satisfied to go along with the status quo."

The others agreed. Auerbach took us to the airport.

Later, Ramsey sided with us and there were many apologies. We were not condemning one waitress, one person, but rather the climate which makes such a thing possible.

The people of Lexington, who had a double standard at that time, were not offended at the game that evening. They got just what they apparently wanted—a lily-white basketball game.

A St. Louis sportswriter, Bob Burns, insisted in his column that I should be suspended and fined for insulting two such fine gentlemen as Ramsay and Hagan.

I wondered then and I wonder now—what about me being insulted? Or am I a person?

Success rode easily with the Celtics. I do not believe we ever became swell-headed. God knows, we had to fight for everything. More often than not crucial series went to the final, gasping minute. Sometimes into overtime.

But, black, white, religious, irreligious, we somehow put together a rather unique example of Americans—a mixed team of men who in forty-eight tumultuous minutes of play could survive it all to go on and win championship after championship.

There were Jews, Catholics, Protestants, agnostics, white men, black men. The one thing we had in common was an Irish name. The Celtics.

Believe me. We did the Irish name proud. Through it all—though I tell truths which may nip occasionally at the heels and the hearts of some members—we never had a clique, we never had a quarrel. A man might be a black super star or a white super star. It made no difference. You might see me, the bomb-thrower, out one night with whites, another night with Negroes, a third night with whites and Negroes. We never considered it unusual. We simply considered ourselves a proud group of men who bore the distinction of being something no one else could be in our sport—the champions of the world.

# CHAPTER VII

# THE PSYCHOLOGY

There was a full house in Kiel Auditorium on that night in December 1956.

The ball went up and Bob Pettit of the Hawks and I jumped for it. I got it and edged it over to Cousy who threw to Heinsohn for a two-point jumper.

"Coon."

"Go back to Africa, you baboon."

"Watch out, Pettit, you'll get covered with chocolate."

"Black nigger."

There was no doubt who the fans were yelling at. I was the only Negro athlete on either team.

If one could query at what moment the string of world championships of the Boston Celtics were born, that would be the one moment which crystallizes in my memory.

St. Louis was a great team at this point. They had Pettit, Hagan, Slater Martin, Ed Macauley, Chuck Share, Alex Hannum, Jack McMahon, the latter two having since become coaches.

But I had a reason. I *always* played well against St. Louis.

There is no point in detailing game by game the sequence of Eastern and world championships which came to the Celtics.

We won in 1957 in double overtime of the seventh and final game. We lost in 1958. We like to think it was because I sprained an ankle in the third game and couldn't play again, except for a brief try. My guys made a tremendous try against St. Louis in that sixth game and just fell short by a point, 110-109.

We lost it.

Then from 1959 on, we never faltered again. Count 'em off. 1959, Minneapolis in four straight—only time it has ever been done. St. Louis in seven games in 1960; St. Louis in five games in 1961; Los Angeles in seven games (and overtime, 110-107) in 1962; Los Angeles in six games in 1963; San Francisco in five games in 1964; Los Angeles in five games in 1965.

That makes eight world championships. There were nine divisional championships. No team—not even the Yankees or the Montreal Canadians—ever had such a streak.

Proud? You bet. Any athlete is proud of a record. The Boston Celtics were proud of a series of championships.

But not fat-headed.

Which were the greatest? To me, the first and the last. The first one was the first professional world championship I had ever won and gave me a thirteen-months' skein which is a kind of unique record for an athlete— a national champion, an Olympic champion and a world professional champion. No one ever did that before. I like it. I admit it.

The first one, then, because it was the first one.

The last one—or, rather, the most recent one, in 1965, because we won it for Walter Brown.

We made the pledge. And we kept it.

In between? Well, they were great championships, but they were never quite the same.

Before beginning some of the true—oh, please, don't call it "inside"—stories of the championships and of the men and the team that made them, I would like to put several false theories to rest.

The first is the philosophy of the fixed game.

Basketball is just like any other sport in the sense that if you are silly enough, you can bet on it.

It is done, as I am sure you know, by a point spread. A team might be a fourteen points favorite. So, automatically if you bet that team you give fourteen points to the other club. Or, conversely, you can take fourteen.

There have been scandals in basketball. However, I would stress—and this is most important—stress, underline, capitalize, that there has never been a scandal in professional basketball.

There never will be. I have heard, just as I am sure you must have, the rumors. Anytime one team upsets another, or winds up breaking even on the points listed by the gamblers, there is a story which goes around:

"They must have had some action."

Ridiculous!

There is not one man in professional basketball who would ever take a chance on bagging a game.

Not because they are all great-hearted. Rather, because it just doesn't make sense.

In order to bag a professional game, you have to put a super star into the deal. Now, a super star is collecting anywhere between $30,000 and $100,000. So how much could you put him down for? $5000? $10,000? Anytime you try to lay that kind of bet every gambler in the country is going to perk up his ears. And how many times can you do it? Once a season? Twice?

Baloney. What's it worth to a super star? You'd have to put yourself in the hands of the gamblers, of the shady people. You'd be risking a lifetime income of a million dollars for a comparative nickel and dime figure, plus your most important possession—a good name.

I do not believe that a professional basketball game can be bagged. I also do not believe that anyone even tries. It is different in colleges. There have been recurrent incidents.

That goes back to what I said earlier about poor kids under pressure. Five grand may look big to a college kid. To a pro, it's the size of one of the pay checks he gets every two weeks over the course of a season.

The other rumor is that the playoffs are sometimes carried over, stretched out as far as possible.

Again, ridiculous!

Unlike pro baseball or football championship shares, which are dependent on attendance, the NBA playoff shares are announced before the semi-finals even start. There is no extra bonus on attendance. You get so much for winning or losing, depending on how far you progress. For example, the Celtics average about $5000 a year for winning. The losers get $3500. We always try to win in four games. We aren't that much in love with the owners that we want to see them get a payday while we sweat and strain. It is worth more—and saves extra plane rides (and we are all afraid of planes)—if you get it over with as fast as possible.

The problems are two-fold. One, you play all season to eliminate one team and then have to fight through the playoffs where every pro is playing his heart out for that one basic motivating ingredient—beautiful, cool, lovely money—and, secondly, the homecourt advantage is an important item in pro basketball because of the proximity of the court to the fans. The referees and the teams are influenced by multi-thousand people yelling and screaming. It's human nature.

Of course, when you take people like me, we enjoy winning on so-called foreign courts. Ah, cad that I am, I have immensely enjoyed watching Doris Day saddened in Los Angeles or Ben Kerner slamming his fist in anger in St. Louis.

But, even in our streak, we didn't win them all on the other court. It's hard to do.

Just plain winning is hard. You are playing against the best there is. In other sports, teams have more players and all the players are not necessarily of the same ability.

In professional basketball, every man has been an All-American in college. There are only eleven—and actually each team plays with its seven best—and when you get the seven best playing out there, you have a game, baby, make no doubt of it.

It's a challenge. And a matter of psychology.

You have to know the right methods and the right movements.

Basically, what you have are ten men in superb condition, on the razor's edge of emotional exhaustion racing up and down the court while 13,909 people yell for blood and two little men with whistles try to make instant judgments about fouls.

If one were to criticize the NBA, it would be about

the referees. There are some good ones. There are some bad ones. But there has never been enough support from the front office to create some kind of overall system of making calls.

Sid Borgia, for example, was the nemesis of the Celtics for years. He had a personal vendetta going with Auerbach and Red wouldn't agree to permit him to referee some key playoff games.

It got out of hand one day in Boston Garden and they stood toe to toe yelling and screaming the most bitter invectives I have ever heard between two men.

That kind of thing hasn't helped the league. Borgia would often call something he said was "common sense." We had another phrase for it. Like one night a guy was coming through the lane and it looked as if there would be a foul for charging or blocking. Borgia blew the whistle before it happened. The man, meantime, had been faked out and had taken steps which automatically gave us the ball. But Borgia said, turning to me: "No foul. You didn't foul him." Then he turned to the guy who walked and said: "And you took steps. But he made you. That's a forced walk. You keep the ball." Forced walk?

Now there's a real psychological problem for you.

There are others, or there were others. One thinks of "Jam-a-day Jimmy Duffy." And Richie Powers, who got so mad in Los Angeles in 1965 that he threw the whistle at Red in a playoff game and said he was quitting. "I won't go for a league where they can vilify you like this without support," he said.

Maybe he was right. You certainly have to consider the ref in this business. It's part of the psychology.

With one ref, you can spend all day inside the twelve-foot foul lane instead of the three seconds allowed. With another, you have to move like a rabbit. With a third, you have to figure he's going to give the edge to the home team and the fourth guy is going to give it to the visiting team, just to prove how tough he is.

Auerbach always insists on having his bench at the backboard where the Celtics will be on defense in the fourth period. His theory is simple. He feels calls against the defense decide the game in the final minutes and he wants to be where he can influence the ref to lay off his group.

I would caution clergy, old ladies, fathers with young daughters, not to get seats behind the Celtics bench for this reason. Arnold is not exactly a shrinking violet when it comes to telling a referee what he thinks.

But it works.

Auerbach's tantrums are probably as much the story of the Celtics as anything else. He does a little war dance when he is wronged. Beautiful. Up, down, in a little circle, stamp the feet, scream, get red in the face, hold the rolled-up program in the air, call the wrath of the gods down on the little men with the whistles.

And the gods—the gallery gods—respond. Heaven help a ref (by the way, have you ever noticed that they have never had a Negro ref?) who antagonizes Red in Boston Garden.

For the player it is a perfect parlay. Red helps us. No doubt of it. Except against some who will call against us, just because he's yelling.

As an insight to the importance of refereeing, let's consider what happened with Philadelphia in the 1965 Eastern finals. Remember now, here are these men playing out the string for a valuable championship. The fans are yelling for blood. The referees are trying to call the game as best they can.

But play starts to get a little out of hand. Gambee, who is known as a cutie, comes in for a rebound and pushes his way through and grabs it. Now Philly takes time out to set up a shot. We're at the other end, boiling mad.

They come in for the shot and maybe I shove someone around, grabbing the rebound. Now, with time running out, it is our ball and we take time out and Philadelphia is romping-stomping mad.

So the ref has let the game get out of hand. Instead of calling it close, he has let an infraction slip by on each side and now the game is going to be rough right until the end, because the tide is running against the referee. The players know he's going to let a lot go and will take advantage of it and are already steamed up to do so.

A referee can also change the complexion of any game

by calling it so tight, that I get three quick fouls. With the limit six, that is going to make me shift my whole style. It is all a matter of judgment.

There has to be some way though that they can pay these referees a decent wage, say $12,000 a year, and give them more security, if they are ever really to take the NBA out of the "Little" league category. Such scenes as that one last year when Powers threw his whistle must cease.

But, as Powers said at the time: "Why should I take this kind of aggravation. No one will support you in the front office. You do a good job and they treat you like you were a thief. You get vilified in the papers and your kids look at you like you were a monster. All for $10,000 a year? Hell, I can make more than that as a salesman."

It happens that Richie Powers was one of the two or three best referees in the NBA today. If he feels that way, then how must the others feel?

Personally, I believe that this hinges on the owners and on the Commissioner. If they want a strong league then they should take a strong stand. Find twelve good referees and pay them good money. Then, maybe —just maybe—they'll straighten out and stop this silliness.

Don't count on it, though. It is liable to go on for a long, long time.

Red is also a judicious judge of the appropriate moment to put in a bullyboy. Loscutoff, for example. He was never smart, but he was strong. Or Bob Brannum, who was before my time, but who they tell me was really tough. Or some of the cuties we've had since.

As I mentioned before, a game can get out of hand when a referee calls it loosely. That's when the players have to use their own psychology of the referee. If he's calling it loose then everyone gets away with more. So, you will have to handle your own man accordingly, unless it's Wilt Chamberlain. Him, you just don't handle. He's too strong. The best you can do is make him work hard.

But, when they call it loose, you jam up on a man a little more, hold him a little tighter.

Of course, a player must be cute to get away with this. Ramsey was our master at drawing a foul. Particularly in the later years of his playing career. Rams would come out wrapped up like a mummy. He was all tape. Breathe on him and he would give you the fallaway, fall-on-the-rump routine and the astonished look. It worked for years. Right up to the time he wrote the piece for *Sports Illustrated* and they tried to fine him $300. President J. Walter Kennedy later called the fine off. Rams never did get many free throws after that.

Loscutoff figured in two funny beef incidents. He made his rep years before when people were pushing Cousy around. Now when you have a super star who is going great, you just have to give him protection or they'll hand him his head.

In a game against New York, Harry Gallatin—then a player—was leaning on Cousy and Loscutoff told him: "Lay off the little guy. He's our bread and butter."

That was before I came. In 1965, Gallatin was coaching New York and he and I had a few words. He was getting ready to throw a punch at Auerbach in a game at Boston Garden and I got mad for one of the few times in my life. I told him: "Gallatin, you've always been a loudmouth fink. Now if you're so tough, why don't you punch me. I'm your size."

Red thought I protected him, but really this is just a thing that grabs you. You get tired of big fatheads picking on little people.

To give you two stories about Loscie, take the 1959 season. Loscutoff ran into Pettit and rode him over his back and Pettit broke his wrist. Loscie was a bit clumsy! Or was he?

Now the next game was in St. Louis and Pettit was out there doing his best and he came in for a layup. Pettit was looking for Loscutoff and Loscie was looking to get out of the way because a foul was crucial. But he was clumsy and he ducked one way and Pettit caromed around him and came too close to the backboard for the layup. He was watching Loscie when he jumped and was a half step too close and, bang, instead of an easy layup, Pettit rammed his head into the under part of the backboard and knocked himself out.

Shows you how lucky you can get.

Also it shows the psychology of playing a pro sport. You always have to be ready to protect yourself.

When you first come into the league they'll always try you out to see if you have the guts for it.

This can consist of any number of things, but mainly it is the rough stuff, pushing, hauling, shoving.

It happened to me and for a few games I forgot about it. The late Jim Krebs of Los Angeles was known in the league as a man who was willing to go beyond the rules in getting his man. He went after me one night in Providence where we played some so-called "neutral court" games every year. Each time he gave it to me, it got worse. The next time he did it, I said: "Krebs. Put your guts where your mouth is."

He threw one punch and I broke his jaw.

They laid off me after that.

In point of fact, I have had only three fights in all my years in basketball and two of them came in the pro ranks.

But, it is part of the psychology of the pros. In college I had only one occasion where a guy had to be straightened out. He came downcourt and gave me an elbow and I said: "Hey baby. You do that and you're going to the hospital."

He made two mistakes. He came back again and he called me a "Black Gorilla." I gave it to him and broke two ribs. It was the only time in my life I intentionally tried to hurt someone.

In college, they stopped elbowing.

In the pros they stopped it, too.

The other two fights I had were with Ray Felix of New York and George Dempsey of Syracuse.

Felix is a player who can be easily upset. One night, on the neutral court of Syracuse, he became upset. He started throwing elbows and I gave him a little shove and the ref called a foul on me.

I turned and was saying to the ref, "That's a good call, Ref, but watch his elbows, will you?" when I saw the ref's eyes going past me. I looked over my shoulder and there was Felix winding up to throw a right hand.

Poor Ray forgot I was left-handed. I started to say, "Hey, wait a minute, baby," but he was already throwing, so I flipped my left into his kisser.

The Dempsey fight was less than that. Syracuse decided to try me out. I guess Dempsey was expendable. He tried. Finally he came at me to dispute the whole affair. He forgot I was left-handed, too, and I started to throw the punch and changed my mind and just sort of hit him with the forearm.

Those who think I'm tough, however, must be quickly apprised of the fact that I am not. There are tough guys in the league. I just try to mind my own business and keep my beautiful kisser intact. But there are times when the psychology of the game demands that you declare yourself.

For those who want fights, there have been plenty. Like the notable incident in Syracuse where they passed the fan around the circle and helped themselves to big chunks of him. He promptly sued them and I believe they paid a final settlement on that last year.

The management uses key fans to keep after the refs and the players as well. This is part of the psychology of pro basketball. Little harassments which can work out.

Philadelphia's Eddie Gottlieb had a fan who sat in the front row beside the bench and rode Auerbach. Finally, one night, they set a play. Cousy was to throw a long pass to Heinsohn. Except that Heinsohn was to duck. Now the Cooz threw that thing pretty hard and you always had to play heads-up ball.

This night, he threw it hard all right and Heinsohn just ducked. The guy in the front row just sort of rolled all his fat up into a heap and we were very solicitous as they lugged him off on the stretcher.

Gentle Jack Nichols—our dentistry student and my sometime roommate—had a doctor's approach to hecklers. That is to say, he sent them to the hospital.

There was a "fan" in a town who always sat in the front row (a plant from the management to rattle us) and was really rough. An avid basketball nut. Except for one thing. He never did notice that Nichols was left-handed.

So, this night, Jack had an out-of-bounds ball and the guy was giving it to Jack pretty good as he stood there with the ball in his left hand. The ref looked upcourt for a split second and Nichols just bounced the ball right off the guy's forehead, recovered it in mid-air and threw it oncourt and started off towards the basket.

At the next time out, the ref asked: "What happened back there?"

"Gee, I dunno," said Nichols. "I think he fainted from the excitement."

Then there was the night when we had an out-of-bounds ball in Philly. The late owner, Ike Richman, held onto it. I guess he was trying to wait until their defense got set. I came after the ball and he wouldn't give it up, so I said very politely:

"Ike, give me the ball or I'll unscrew your head and throw that out there."

Play resumed.

Oh, I tell you, it's a fun league, this NBA.

To capsulize it, though, there are some unwritten rules. Like never throwing an elbow straight out. As I said, I put a guy in the hospital in college that way and there have been plenty of examples in the pros as well. I can say honestly now that if you ever see me out there with my elbows spread as I come down for a rebound that it means just one thing—the game is getting rough and dirty and I am letting them know that I am becoming a little burned up about it.

Another rule we have: Try not to put your fingers in the other man's eye. We trim fingernails, except for one or two offenders. Losing an eye is a prevalent hazard of the league. Oscar Robertson is a case in point. He nearly lost his eye last year.

I nearly lost mine in the final game of the 1965 playoffs against Los Angeles. I had been accidentally speared in the first quarter, and I could not see out of my left eye throughout the remainder of the game.

As a result, I spent the following ten days in bed not moving my head because the doctors thought I might lose the sight of that eye.

And it was all the result of an unintentional accident.

That's the way it goes. You are big guys and playing

for money and it makes for accidents. As long as they are not intentional, it is just an occupational hazard.

There are many other psychological points as well. Several of these I will not mention lest I lead the youth of America astray. They can learn them when they get in the pros.

You might be interested in the exchanges which go on when you are playing against a super star, though.

For example, let us take Chamberlain. Wilt Chamberlain of the Philadelphia 76'ers. You take him. I've had enough of him.

Seriously, Wilt and I have never engaged in any rough stuff. Perhaps the closest we ever came was that memorable incident in 1964 in Boston when Auerbach came running up from the bench and started a vehement altercation with Wilt at midcourt.

For years, we all wondered what would happen if Wilt ever got mad. We figured it was a case of just running out of the hall, because Chamberlain just has to be the strongest man alive. Sam Jones had a small beef with him once and Sam ran back to the bench and picked up a stool to defend himself. We were in sympathy with Sam, who is not exactly short on courage. Fortunately, Wilt cooled down.

In this particular game, Wilt wasn't cooling off. He had just plain and simply had enough, between transferring to San Francisco and getting a lot of bad raps and one thing and another, and Red came up to exchange remarks.

Red was within four feet of Wilt on the sidelines as I ran up. I put my hand out on Wilt's arm and yelled, "Get back, Red, you're six inches too close."

Auerbach, yelling all the while, took one giant step back and at the same time Chamberlain just shook my hand off with one sweep.

I thought: "Okay, Wilt, if that's the way you feel, then go ahead."

At this unhappy moment, along came Clyde Lovellette. Clyde was a big, big man and he and Wilt had been swapping beefs for years. Clyde came up from Wilt's flank and said something and put his hands up, but there was a slip between the fist and the face. Wilt just sort of poked out that right hand and Clyde went to one knee and stayed there, carefully considering the rivets in the floor and wondering why the floor was tilting.

We found out what we wanted to know—Chamberlain can hit.

It was Clyde's major contribution of the 1964 season. Frankly, I was only surprised that it took Chamberlain so many years to clout Clyde.

I suppose it is also time to get out of the way the major issue of Chamberlain versus Russell.

No faults from me, baby.

He and I have passed the stage where we can "psych" each other.

There were times, perhaps, when a little psychology was in order, but they are long since gone. The closest it can come now is like in the 1965 playoffs when we were going hammer and tongs at each other and I said: "I never thought I would see the day when you would push me."

To which he replied: "Cut that out, baby. You ain't psyching me."

It may be the so-called "man to man clash" that the sportswriters like to refer to, but actually, when I play Chamberlain, I play a team. Wilt, conversely, plays his game and the others fall into his wake and are swept along. The theory of playing against Chamberlain is to keep the ball from him as much as possible.

Chamberlain's physical power is awesome. Most certainly he can jump higher from a crouch than any man in the league. He is a good shooter as well and shoots as finely as any pivotman in professional basketball, using that fallaway jumper. Of course, he doesn't have a touch like a Sam Jones or Robertson or Jerry West, but they are exceptions.

Still, Chamberlain came into the league in 1959-60 and from that moment Russell had a big challenge on his hands. The theory was that Chamberlain was going to ruin my style of defense. Few realized that we play an entirely different kind of game. Chamberlain's concept of the game is basically offensive—the style, that is. In this area of psychology of the game, there are many facets. One of these is Auerbach's stringent adherence to the rule—never say anything which will steam up an opponent or another team as a unit.

It is a good bit of psychology.

At the same time, you paid good money for this book. Ergo, you should get the truth, regardless of psychology

Therefore, the truth about my major individual opponent—Wilt Chamberlain. Does he frost me? Do I dislike him? Did I consider him the big challenge of my life?

Answers: No. No. And, not any more.

Reasons:

Chamberlain came into the league and was supposed to put me into total eclipse. I think he has had the opposite effect. In a sense, he has magnified my importance to the team.

We have always been friends, except on a basketball court. There, he wears a different uniform, and he and all others like him are my sworn enemies.

For one thing, I owe a debt of gratitude to Chamberlain. He made me a $100,001 a year ballplayer. I had an idea in my mind that I was going to get close to a hundred dred gees after the 1965 season.

Auerbach took over as G.M. of the Celtics on Brown's death and exercised a long-standing option to buy ten percent of the club at its book value of $1,500,-000. In other words, he put up about $150,000. It was a smart deal. Mrs. Brown and Lou Pieri were going to sell the team. What were you going to buy? As Eddie Powers long before said to the Internal Revenue in those dark, dread days of near bankruptcy, all you were buying were ten used jockstraps and a bottle of aspirins. The team couldn't be sold without having Auerbach involved in the deal.

When the team was sold, Ruppert Knickerbocker paid $3,000,000. Auerbach therefore made a cool $150,000 capital gains profit. He also signed on for five years at $55,000 per as G.M. and coach (with the option of being coach for only one year if he so desired) and received further executive options.

I was glad for him. It was a long way from Brooklyn. I had teased him for years that I was going to play until I found him getting ulcers either from me or from the Chinese food he gulps down (I mean, this has to be a strange man who will have Chow Mein and a Coke for breakfast).

But I had made some good investments and the time was coming when I should quit. I halfway made up my mind that I would quit that summer. But, of course, Ruppert Knickerbocker wasn't about to want that. They bought the jockstraps and they wanted someone to fill them.

Enter Bill Russell with a pleasant subject on his mind—money.

They offered, through Auerbach, $75,000. I said I was going to consider retiring. They stuck at $75,000. I considered retiring. (In the meantime, I made two appearances at the World's Fair for Schaefer Beer. Oh, traitor. The shame of it. And I don't even drink.)

Now, we went up to Kutshers for the annual Maurice Stokes Charity Game and while we were there, Philadelphia announced that Wilt Chamberlain had signed a contract for three years at $100,000 per year.

Good for Wilt Chamberlain.

And good for Bill Russell. I just smiled and laughed and was happy as hell. If Chamberlain was worth $100,-000, then I figured on the basis of all those championships I was worth just $1 a year more.

Frankly, we went right to the wire. You seldom get an insight into the contractual dealings of pro ballplayers. Most of them tell you lies.

I've heard all kinds of stories about how much money baseball players really made as opposed to their announced salaries, such as the claims about one player getting one hundred thousand, followed by a legal case revealing he actually received $60,000.

On my score, you can count it anytime you want to talk to the Internal Revenue. One hundred thousand—and one—dollars.

Red offered me everything but the kitchen sink (and no raise). Stock tips. This thing and that thing.

I said: "Red, baby. You got yours. I get mine. Either I'm worth a buck more than Chamberlain or I'm not."

I was.

Thank you, Wilt Chamberlain.

You might call the foregoing part of the psychology of the game. You hear so much baloney about guys playing the pro game because they love it and all that jazz. I love it. But, I tell you no lies. I am thirty-one years old and I play it for money, too. Perhaps in the area of much more significant accomplishment, I can do something when I retire.

In the area of psychology let me further add that I play it every game just as best I can. I have seen men in many sports who play it only according to the schedule.

In my mind, the schedule is every game. And that's that. Here's the way I look at it. I am a professional ball player. I am paid because people pay to see me play. Therefore, I must give them forty-eight minutes worth of the best game I have, regardless of whether we are playing for the world championship, or just playing out the string in early March, after we've already won the regular season title. The fan deserves it. It costs him an average of four dollars for a ticket, four dollars I assume you worked hard to earn. I am earning my money. It's that simple.

It doesn't make me a great guy. Just a pro.

Conversely, in the psychology of the game, or at least in the psychology of the role of a so-called sports super star, I don't believe that the fan has the right to intrude on my privacy. Therefore I am not happy when I am out eating with my family or carrying on a private conversation with a friend and some perfect stranger sits down with me and starts telling me how great he and I are, asking for my autograph.

I rarely give autographs. It is just the way I am. I cannot imagine the value of a scribbled name on a piece of paper. It does not make me popular. I mean, every pro super star is supposed to come ready-made out of a package of All-American boy Wheaties . . . oops, pardon me, Ruppert Knickerbocker.

Now what value can my signature possibly have? And why should I have to sign it? I give my money's worth on a playing court. If I want to do something charitable, either by financial donation or by making a visit to a hospital, I do not require that nine cameramen and four writers tell the world what a great guy I am.

I am me. Period. I am public property when I play. I am private property when I am not playing.

If I want to sign, I will. But no one has ever forced me to do anything. You either buy me as Bill Russell, man, or you don't. My signature isn't going to make any difference. And the fact that I am a basketball player is just an accident.

I would much rather have been a major contributor like Salk or Stevenson. I've met some of them. I have never asked them for their autographs. I have never judged them as great men on their ability to write their name.

And how about these guys who give you fourteen stories about how they don't want the autograph for themselves, but for their eleven-year-old nephew. I mean, I don't care, baby. If you really need it to get by with then I'll give it, but please, spare me the details about who wants it.

Autograph hunters can be fantastic.

Like, I'm sitting in a movie one night, all by myself. I'm sitting in the center of the theater row in downtown Detroit, minding my own business. Along comes a guy and sits down beside me. The whole row is empty, but he sits beside me. Thirty minutes pass and I have half an eye on the movie and half an eye on this guy. Finally he says: "Can I have your autograph?"

Oh baby. Beautiful. I was so relieved I signed it.

Take the end of the 1964 season. It had been a tough year and my wife and I decided to get away from it all for awhile. We went to New Hampshire and checked into a nice, quiet motel and had a nice, quiet dinner and sat around and watched TV. We went to bed late and I was enjoying the first sound sleep I had had in a month when the phone rang at 9 A.M.

It was the motel switchboard operator. She wanted me to know that the guests were waiting outside my room for me to come out and sign autographs and I was delaying their departure.

I mean, can she be serious? What is this, anyway? But it happens all the time.

And not just to me. Chamberlain was eating dinner one night and a lady was going to hit him with her pocketbook because he said, "Excuse me, but could I sign later? My steak is getting cold." It took Dolph Schayes to pull her away.

Oh yes, pardon the diatribe. Back to Wilt the player. He is big. He is strong. He is a nice guy with a pancreatic problem, who is becoming richer and richer and, if I were to sum up his one problem, I would say that at seven feet his biggest difficulty is that people expect him to be Superman. But he isn't. He's just a man.

I have had a long series with Wilt, I have respect for him. And a liking. But he came in to dominate this NBA.

He is a great one. In his first year, he was starting All Star on the East team. He was Most Valuable Player of the Year, First Team all leagues. Wilt played with Tom Gola and Guy Rodgers and Woody Sauldsberry and Paul Arizin. You couldn't find greater teammates. But the Celtics were champions.

One of the handicaps of playing in the league is, it's so full of All Americans. Regard any of the great stars and remember and ask: How many played on national championship teams in college? Very few.

Then you come into the pros and it is a case of the coach either making you play the team's game—a little matter of psychology—or the coach making the team play your game.

When I came into the league, Auerbach told me one thing: "Never mind making points. Just get me the ball." That is testimonial to Arnold Auerbach's ability to be a coach.

For the rest, what can I say for Wilt Chamberlain? Remember now, Auerbach says never knock anybody, never say even the stray thing which may upset an opponent.

I don't know what Auerbach's putting in his book. But in mine, truth.

Chamberlain is a great opponent. He has had his

problems. Sure, he has pushed a little. Sure, he has run with the ball a little. Sure, he gets away with a violation on the three-second rule.

That's the fault of the refs.

The fact that others play his game is the fault of the coach. He was my great challenge. He won his awards. I won mine. To me, the great awards were the championships.

For myself, I think it can be said—or, at least, I have the guts to say it—I think I may not be now, but in my past nine years I was the best player in the NBA. Not the first months when I started, but certainly after my first season.

But that's my "humble" opinion.

Also, it can be written that Bill Russell says of Wilt: "He's a fink."

I hasten to add that the Bill Russell in question is my son, not me.

As Wilt said before we played that last game in the Eastern finals in 1965:

"You've played a great series, Russ."

I could have added: "So did you." But I was thinking: "I wish you got hit by a car on the way to the game."

I have my own rules on psychology. I hate no one. And, in fact, though I talk about money, I never played a really big game for $$ because you just don't talk about it. It is not just money. It is far more important. It is the challenge and the pride of being a world champion and of playing for it.

Perhaps, in the final essence, that is the true psychology. A band of men playing for a goal. Just a bunch of men, who understand each other's faults, going flat out for the championship.

Maybe, when you hit *that* point, you have touched upon the true beauty of sports.

We certainly touched it last year. We came right to the final game in the Easterns with Philadelphia. The seventh game. It went into the last second, but this was before the game. A moment for a great psychologist to say something.

Maybe this can stand for the ultimate in psychology:

The locker-room before this last game. 13,909 wild fans inside. 10,000 people storming the gates. Players staring off into space. Russell throwing up. LeRoux winding and rewinding tape. Heinsohn sneaking a smoke. K.C. Jones looking straight ahead. Sam Jones retying a shoelace for the twenty-first time. Havlicek fiddling with his knee brace again. Auerbach, deep pouches in his eyes, a ragged, dirty cigar poking out of his mouth, chewing the dead lip of it.

The knock came on the door. The Celtics dynasty might be over. Auerbach looked up, sprawled in the chair, looking for all the world like a fugitive from a wake. "Win or lose," he said, "you're still my team."

We started towards the door and someone looked back and said: "Lose? Are you kidding me, baby?"

I believe it could be called psychology.

# CHAPTER VIII

## THE CHAMPIONSHIPS

It was April 17, 1965, at Boston Garden. We were playing the Philadelphia 76'ers for the Eastern championships. It was the seventh and final game. We had blown a game in Philly two days earlier in the very final second of play when Hal Greer took an out-of-bounds pass and made a great, swishing basket.

Now, it was for the championship. And it looked bad. All through the game we made runs for it and every time Chamberlain and Greer and the rest of them closed in on us again. We couldn't shake them. Finally, we clambered into a, gulp, one point lead. We had led by six, but we dissipated it. We were sitting on the lead, holding it. It didn't work.

Philadelphia made a mistake. The ball went out of bounds and we fought for it.

It was our ball, three seconds remaining. I had it behind my own basket. All I had to do was throw it in to Sam Jones or Johnny Havlicek and the world championship was virtually ours (we were scheduled to play L.A., but Baylor was hurt and we knew it would be no trouble).

I was being guarded by Chet Walker. I took my time and then threw the ball in. It hit the guy-wire which supports the basket and Philadelphia grabbed it. They took time out.

All in one breath, I was yelling at the referee, down on one knee, slamming the floor with my fist, the Celtics bench was emptying around me, 13,909 people were going mad and—they told me later—the Celtics announcer

Johnny Most could only scream into the mike: "He hit the wire . . . he hit the wire . . . he hit the wire."

He did indeed.

What did I say? I yelled to the referee that Walker had his foot over the out-of-bounds marker and that he hit the ball with his hand. Later, movies showed that he had been over the line, but he didn't hit it. The ball did definitely hit the wire—which, incidentally, wasn't supposed to be there, but the Garden was saving money.

Be that as it may, I yelled at the ref. Then I went on my knees. I knew instinctively what to say. What does a super star say in a moment of crisis? What great leadership does he show?

I just slammed my fist into the court and said: "Oh my God . . . oh, my God . . . it's their ball."

It certainly was, and on the basis of what they did two days earlier it was their ball game, because in the NBA one or two seconds is a phenomenally long, long time.

There was time out while they set the play. We knew what it had to be—Greer. Shoot! Or, Chamberlain. Stuff!

What do you do about it? What great plays do you make? I'll tell you. We stood in the semi-circle around Auerbach. In the broadcasting cage Johnny Most kept saying: "Yes, he did. He did. He hit the wire. By God, he hit the wire."

18,000 people screamed.

But we were measuring up to the moment. World champions. Pro ballplayers. We knew just what to say. What did we say? Nothing. Absolutely nothing.

Red just stood there, all pale and sick (who wasn't?). He looked up at us and said: "So, what do we do now?"

Who knew? The whole sequence of all the world championships and Eastern championships and the records and everything else had come down to the final second. You're a bum or you're not.

We felt like bums. The lost sheep of the NBA. Oh, my God. Do we have to go out there and face this?

I thought: "Now all summer 50,000 people are going to ask me: What did you think when you hit the wire?"

But we had to go through with it. The ball went to Greer out of bounds. It had to be one of two plays.

115

Either they threw it in to Chamberlain for a stuff or Greer threw it in bounds then cut and recovered for a set shot. Either was death with that ball at this point.

Chamberlain squared off with me. Did we exchange words? What bon mot passed between us? He just looked me in the eye. I just looked back. We were under the backboard. From his eyes I knew it was going to be his play. I got ready to put my weight against his. For all the marbles. For all the money and the years, good and bad, the MVP trophies and the All Star Games and all the rest of it. For the whole career.

I thought: "Well, Russell. Let's see what kind of man you are now." I couldn't hear the crowd. In my ears it was deathly still. I couldn't see anything but his eyes.

Greer lobbed the ball in and Chamberlain planted himself and got ready for the throw which was to come from Walker. Walker put his hands up for it and just at that last split, flashing second Havlicek came out of nowhere, facing Walker with his hands up the way he flags them when he hopes against hope he will block a pass, and the ball just lobbed right off his extended arm and into the hands of Sam Jones.

I saw it all in the flash of a second.

Sam—the great, put-the-money-on-the-line clutch player—had the ball and was dribbling it to the other end of the court and all of a sudden there were 18,000 people coming at us and the game was over and we were Eastern champions again and, undoubtedly in our minds, world champions, and then they were lifting us on their shoulders and I was being trampled and shoved and someone was tearing Havlicek's shirt off and Auerbach was on and off shoulders and looked like he was lost and maybe frightened as the mob pulled in. Chamberlain was just disappearing behind this wave of people and I saw his eyes and looked kind of blank at him and he looked blank back and disappeared into the limbo of another frustration and we were being dragged off to the locker-room.

There was no elation. There was no feeling of victory. Suddenly, there was emptiness. Eighteen thousand people were cheering. My teammates were jumping around with joy. Havlicek's shirt was being torn off and there was a frightened look in his eyes as the mob came at him.

And for myself there was only the vague emptiness and the feeling of despair. Another victory. Another vanquished opponent. And you wonder—how can grown men, players and fans, pour so much of themselves into a game? Just a game. Just a minute, a second, a flash, an unimportant moment in relation to the world. What does this game mean? Does it win a big victory for the human race? Does it make us all better men?

But they pat you on the back and they mean well and they are wild and enthused and you go down the runway and once again you are the champion.

That was the end of one segment of another season.

That was the way it was.

That is the way it is.

The champions.

By the grace of an extended arm. You play all season for the moment and when it hits you it is virtually an unbelievable thing, one you can't cope with.

It takes days to settle down again.

When we did settle down we almost toyed with Los Angeles for our eighth world championship. They didn't have Baylor and without him they were exposed, beatable. West was going to play his usual great game. But we weren't about to lose.

We won the first two games in Boston with so much ease that it was enough to make us cocksure as we flew out to L.A. Then we lost. Bang. We were awful. Doris Day jumped up and down with happiness. Dean Martin laughed with glee. Peter Falk, friend of Auerbach, frowned. We reversed the procedure in the fourth, winning easily. Now we headed home.

Farewell, Hollywood. L.A. flew back at the front of the plane (one thing I'll say for the Lakers, owner Bob Short never made them travel cheap). We flew back in our usual tourist arrangement. Back to Boston, leading 3-1.

Boston Garden has a fire law crowd of 13,909. They must have had 18,000 people there. It was like a rising tide, a roaring crescendo. Above us hung a banner—

"Celtics 1." It was for Walter Brown. We promised something on September 7, 1964, when he died.

It figured. In the fourth period we got the fast break going and we rolled, scoring twenty-one points while L.A. managed none. The Celtics put on the most fantastic rush that has ever been seen in a championship competition and just ran off with it.

We didn't even realize what was happening. Before the game we were as race horses must be, waiting for the bell. We went out on the court tense, but knowing we were going to win. No grand words. No pledges in the locker-room.

The people yelled and the sound came at us like waves and the first half was tough and then suddenly as the final period began it was fantastic. I put my hand up and a ball was in it and I threw to Sam Jones. I put my hand out and there was another ball and I threw to K.C. Jones and he made it. I put my hand out and there was another ball and I threw to Havlicek and he made it. I threw and threw and blocked and threw and the team— the world champion Boston Celtics—*was* a team. Every game we ever played meshed together and we didn't even know the score or that we were shutting them out. We just knew shoot, run, block, pass, shoot.

Then it became frightening. More than a mere sports event. We were not just beating this team. We were destroying it. The people were screaming. They were yelling for blood. It was like the Colosseum of Rome. They were yelling for all their frustrations, all their pent-up feelings about the world. They were egging us on to destroy, to kill, to reduce an opponent to nothing.

And we were responding. We were, in a basketball sense, killing them, leaving them shattered among the ashes of their pride.

We were running over them like a man might run over a floundering cripple with his car.

Compelled. Unable to stop. Meshing together all the years and running like a precise, perfect machine.

It was my worst moment in sports. There was the horror of destruction, not the joy of winning. The horror of knowing you are the instrument of the voices of man calling out:

"Destroy . . . kill . . . ruin."

We ruined them. Two minutes into the fourth, we were so far in front that we could not be caught. Yet, we were all silent. The long road had come to a fearful end. We knew—and did not know—we sensed, and did not completely comprehend, that we had taken sports out of the realm of a game.

Only Heinsohn of our old original championship gang was on the bench. Tommy was retiring. He was going out without playing and he deserved better, because he was a great star and a great clutch player and a great champion. But for him, the echoes of the cheers were already distant and part of the past.

We felt for him. Red said later he wouldn't let him go off to a thunderous ovation because he thought Heinsohn didn't deserve to go off playing with subs. A matter of judgment. For, by that time, Auerbach could afford to take us all out. I came out with ten minutes left, the earliest I had ever been out of a championship game. I sat there and laughed with all the rest as the tension ebbed. The crowd was not ferocious now. Now they, too, were calm, laughing, sated with what they had seen.

I came out and I put my hand out towards Auerbach and he was dancing up and down and laughing with the traditional program still wrapped in his hand, but laughing, laughing, and I put my hand out and he shook it and I hugged him and we were kings of the world, not professional basketball players but a beautiful, skilled team and we were the champions and then we sat on the bench and laughed as the kids played the Lakers and we were winning handily and the gun went off and the people came after us.

We always dunk Red in the shower and he had stripped his watch and emptied his pockets and he sat there as we came down the stretch, laughing, talking, happy, with poor Tom Heinsohn—our guy, our teammate who had counted so much through all the ferocious moments—sitting back with arms folded, headed into retirement without a cheer.

The gun went off and it was over and the people came at us out of everywhere and I almost broke my foot getting it caught in the bench, and they overwhelmed us and carried us off and as we went towards the dressingroom I looked up and I saw the banner: "Celtic 1" and I raised my hand. Everyone wondered why later.

I was raising it to a man. "So long, Mr. Brown. Like we promised. There's your championship."

That was where it ended. For the purposes of this book, which is written between the 1965 and 1966 season, that is also where it ends.

It begins long before.

Back in 1957 when we won the first championship. A long time ago. A lot of plane rides. A lot of tension. A lot of laughs.

A lot of world championships.

A lot of lonely months.

That was supposed to be the title of this book—*Seven Lonely Months*. Perhaps better than anything else it would tell the story of the men who engage in professional sports—or, even, any profession—in this United States of the 1960s.


I came to Boston in December, you'll recall, and I came in under a pressure. For one thing, there were many who thought I couldn't make it in the league. For another, there was the built-in pressure of being the first of the so-called "giant super stars." In my case, I was six feet, ten inches tall, and a Negro. And I began wearing a beard, just to be different.

After the first season, I let Heinsohn shave my goatee off in the celebration over the world championship.

The next year I just grew it back. People have commented on the beard ever since. It has become the *cause célèbre* of the NBA. Everyone says: "He could be a nice guy. Why doesn't he shave that beard?"

Now how can that have any effect on whether I am a nice guy or not?

I grew my beard because when I was a rookie I had never shaved. Heinsohn shaved it when we won the first world championship.

I grew it back because I wanted to. I wear it maybe just to let people know that I am an individual. I am me. It's just something I want to do. It's part of me.

I mean, do we knock Mitch Miller?

Or, at least, do we knock him because he has a beard?

Arnie Risen was the center in 1957. Arnie was getting older and I was the rookie who was taking his place.

He plunged right in to help me out.

It was entirely different from the usual situation on a professional team. I remember Y. A. Tittle telling one time about when he broke in on the San Francisco 49'ers. Tittle asked a well-known quarterback something about certain plays and the quarterback just smiled and said: "Baby, you're after my job. You find out."

That has never been the case with the Celtics. The atmosphere of everyone helping out was part of the success which came to this team and when my time comes I will do the same thing for the guy who is going to take my place. That's just the way it is.

Joining the team, I immediately implemented an inner decision which I had made. I would speak only when spoken to. I would not be unfriendly, but at the same time I did not want the reputation of being just a joking, laughing Negro.

As the only Negro on the team I sensed—right or wrong—that I would have to prove myself as a man over a long period of time.

It has always been that way with me and it always will be. I never in my life consciously worked to be liked. I work only to be respected.

It was hard work to reach that goal.

There were the sneers in St. Louis. The lonely months. The knowledge that around the league everyone was going to take a try at me to see how tough I was, to see if I could cut it.

After one game with New York, Gallatin told a writer: "How good is he? See me in four or five years when he's been around for a while. Then we'll see how good he is."

I smiled to myself.

Gallatin gave me a good shoving around. I felt my way through it. I thought: "It's just one game. We'll see next time. I learned he was cute. Now we'll see how cute he is next time."

In St. Louis, I was alone. Nobody went anywhere with me. Jack Nichols, who was studying dentistry, was my roommate, but Jack made very few of the trips. St. Louis was the loneliest town in the world.

After the coffee-shop closed, there was only one place to get anything to eat. It was a rundown joint across the street and all the players went in there. But not Bill Russell. Rundown or not, I couldn't be served there.

So I went hungry.

And angry.

But no person in the world was ever going to chase me out of basketball or out of life.

In college I had been called a "big, black gorilla." I was called it just once by that guy with the elbows. No one ever tried it again.

But in St. Louis it was "baboon . . . nigger . . . black gorilla." Not from the players. Never have I heard a professional ballplayer say anything about race in a game. But the fans were using it as a weapon.

What do you say in the face of prejudice?

You don't say anything. You just play . . . and act like a man.

I felt it. I told my wife that you just couldn't let a town like St. Louis beat you. It's me against the world. "I'll never be a big star in Boston, a big sports hero like Williams or Cousy," I said. "I'm a Negro and I might as well face it."

Cousy was the captain of the 1957 team. He went his way and I went mine. There was no personality conflict involved. Later, as the years passed, Cooz and I would occasionally play in the same card game and occasionally say a few words. It was a remote relationship, although I had deep respect for him and believe he returned it for me. In fact, Cousy could do some things which were very pleasant surprises.

Still, throughout, it had to be the lonely life. The long trips, the long hours, the walls closing in on you late at night when you are alone and tense and have no one to be with, no one to talk to, to laugh with, to argue with.

And the certain knowledge that within the boundaries of this league regardless of how it went it would be an uphill fight. I would never become the super star.

Yet, I knew that given enough years the barriers could be broken. Strange? Yes. Hurt? Yes. Hurting? Yes. Striking out? Sometimes. I am not the same man today that

I was then. I believed everything I said then. I have changed some views over the years, but circumstances have changed as well. But through it all I clung to my own belief that you must speak the truth as the truth appears to be at that time.

And you must play the best kind of basketball possible.

In my case that was defense. Auerbach told me at the start not to think about shooting. "Your game is to get me the ball. You get the ball and throw it up there for the shooters. We'll count rebounds as baskets for you."

So we started counting rebounds. We drew great crowds and we were rolling and everywhere we went the gauntlet was cast down and challenge was made. I was pushed. I pushed back. I was shoved. I shoved back. I started a little book on players, a mental thing. Who has to shoot righthanded? Who is only a shooter and a ball-hog and won't pass? Can I psych them?

The Celtics never really have had any particularly different plays. We work off a basic pattern of about seven which, with options, can amount to about thirty. For codes we sometimes use fingers or just a stray word as we pass a man by. If we saw that Cousy was loose, I might say "New York" to him, or he might say it to me and we would know that this would be a play where he was to cut from his man and move to the left for an open shot from the flank.

We began to learn to work together and we began to learn more and more about defense.

Auerbach was an innovator. He would let the athletes run their own plays. As time went on other teams tried time and again to set up different patterns to break up the threat off the boards. They would almost always overplay on me, thus shaking someone else loose and we would exploit it time and again.

At that same time, there was the constant recurrent battling with the old pros. The league has changed a lot since. But in those days you either fought, or they ran you right out of the league. I was not exactly passive. I gave as good as I got.

I had one big edge going—the blocked shot.

To this moment, I could not teach anyone the practical application of the blocked shot. It must first be understood that according to the old school this is fundamentally very poor defense.

Auerbach recognized it for what it was. Properly applied it was as much psychological as actual.

You must learn just when a player is going to shoot; what type of shot he has, and where you have to be to block it. You have to know exactly where you are on the floor at all times. And you have to develop by repetition until it becomes almost second nature. I call it "canned thinking." It is right there when I want it.

Let's face it. You can only block a shot ten or twenty percent of the time. I don't know at what given moment that percentage will come true. Neither does the shooter.

A sixth sense is developed for it and a quick move at the same time knowing just what the habits of the opponent are. Your man develops these habits over the years and so you have to learn to make them do what you want them to do; make them switch from their accustomed habit into something new where they are instinctively uncomfortable. If you can do that, then you have them halfway beaten. If the guy likes to go left, then make him go right. If he likes the foul line shot, then make him go two feet further back.

To categorize it, look at defense on this basis:

(1) Learn the other man's habits. Then make him go exactly opposite to what he likes to do.

(2) When he gets to a position where he is away from his best shot, even if it's only a foot, make him commit himself and shoot and count on the law of averages being on your side.

(3) If you're successful, just smile at him as though you can do it every time.

I believe this is called "applied psychology" . . . or practical psychology.

Now, if there are three guys or two coming at you on a fast break, you must work on the same basic system.

The first thing, make them slow up and stop. The second is make them throw a bad, hurried pass. The third is make them commit on a bad shot. The fourth is—block the ball.

If you can ever find anyone who can do all that with regularity, quit work and start your own basketball team.

Seriously, let's say that is happening and the middle man has the ball. Now, I want the right hand man to take the shot, because I know he's a little out of position. So I move towards the player with the ball and give him enough fake motion to make him stop and look and at the same time I move towards the left so that he thinks the man on the right is free. Then as soon as he is committed I am already turning and moving to the man on the right to hurry his shot and am in position to block it. They are committed. If nothing worse, I get the rebound and I turn back again to throw the ball up court.

For years, the Celtics used the fast break, but to me the best team we ever had was in 1964-1965, when we were so strong on defense. Let's face it. We are all former All-Americans in the NBA. The emphasis has been on scoring throughout our careers. But, if I score twelve points and my man who normally averages twelve, scores eighteen, then I am giving away six points and I am a failure. That is how I look at it and it's also how the Celtics, under the coaching of Auerbach, have always looked at it.

Defense must be learned over many years. You can never play in the NBA unless you learn it. Many is the kid who came in and left after training camp because he just couldn't comprehend how to do it.

Things like learning never to cross your legs when running—a very natural tendency—but instead to glide like a crab. Or taking abnormal steps and running backwards. And learning how to guard your man and keep him from the ball, or else so harried that he can't do anything with it.

Rebounding is different. Here, in the snakepit, you must have position. Three-quarters of all rebounds are taken below the rim, so you have to learn the precise moment to go for the ball. After all, in a league of giants, anyone can go above the rim.

You have to learn how to give a second effort as well. Many rebounds are caught after six or seven tries. I have always practiced—fortunately, I don't need it any more—jumping continually at the backboard until I

125

could go up to the rim thirty-five times without stopping. If you build your timing and your legs like that over the years you have an edge.

It takes strong legs and strong hands, because you have to fight for the ball. I still remember the time when one of our strongest men, Gene Conley, decided to fight Chamberlain for the ball. He grabbed it and hung on and Chamberlain just lifted him and the ball right up towards the rim.

The super stars—the Baylors, Pettits, Robertsons, Wests—will conversely keep trying to make you do what they want. That is where the concentration comes in on defense. If they can get you into their position you are dead. They'll kill you every time. So, you must stay between the man and the ball and keep him from getting it. If he does get it, you must harass him and worry him so that he will get rid of it in a hurry and be out of position.

There are other elements. Sometimes, I will let a man get away with something in two or three games. Then, I'll just move in on him.

There he is fat-catting, figuring that he has me beat. He figures he's the guy that's going to run Russell out of the league. Nobody runs me out, baby. I'll leave when I get good and ready, and I just move in and give him a "Wilson-burger" which is the name we developed for stuffing a ball back down their throat.

I might stuff it at him and ask: "Ketchup or mustard?"

Or a rookie will say: "I'm coming through, Russ."

I'll say back: "I'll be there waiting for you, sweetheart,"

One time there was a kid—Tom Hoover of New York —who thought he really had me beat. He was using a play which I had in high school. For two games I let him go. We won both games and I was setting him up.

Now, in the third game he started giving me the romance and I fed him a "Wilson-burger."

"What's doing, kid?" I said. "What do you think this is, amateur night? I was using that play when you were in grammar school. Heck, I invented it."

He never did completely recover. He's always looking over his shoulder for me. He often finds me there.

Conversation between players is normal. Here are ten

126

men on the verge of hysteria running up and down a court chasing a ball and naturally enough they are going to exchange words. Sometimes it's a warning. Sometimes it's a joke.

Chamberlain was trying to take hooks on me one night. They weren't going in. We ran past each other. I said: "Why don't you try kicking it in?"

Robertson was coming down for a shot and went around me. "Take it easy on me, big fella. Give me a break," he said. I just looked at him. He had forty points. He grinned and he ran back upcourt.

A new player starts testing himself, pushing in the snakepit under the boards. "Oh," I say. "You're a big old pusher now, huh? Going to pick on the poor old man. Going to pull my beard. Tsk . . . tsk. I'm not that old." Then I shove him real hard.

Chico Vaughn of St. Louis is a good kid. But you have to keep on these kids and give them the psyching bit.

He was driving in a lot on me in one game. "I'm coming through, Russ," he said. Then I just smiled and blocked his shot:

"Oh, this is nothing. Next time, bring some salt and pepper. I'm really going to feed you basketballs, baby."

Part of the game.

Or Walt Bellamy of New York will hold and shove and push a little too much and the referee will call it. Bellamy will say: "Hey, Mr. Ref., Mr. Chamberlain does it. Mr. Russell does it. What am I, a nothing?"

It breaks me up every time.

Once, Bellamy went on with that routine and was quite vociferous against "Mr. Referee," who turned and said:

"Well, I tell you what, sir. You just tell Mr. Bellamy that Mr. Referee said that that last remark is going to cost him $25 because Mr. Bellamy has just been given a technical fine."

But if it all sounds like fun, it's not. It is high-speed applied psychiatry. It is a fight to the finish, a capsulized forty-eight-minute version of a guerrilla war or the struggles and hates and frustrations and successes of a lifetime. Basketball is probably the most emotional game in the world.

Soccer is equally emotional, as witness the riots overseas. But the fans are separated from the playing surface in soccer. Here in the United States, basketball fans are as much a part of the game as the players.

As I've said previously, we often will be playing to the fans—or with them. Hence, one gets the image of the home-court advantage which is not a myth, but a fact.

And the image of the bush league. When pro basketball began it was the short subject of sports entertainment, the event which went on just before the dance. The owners lugged their office around in their pocket.

Too much of that has still carried over. Right from the start, we learned about playing the fans from Auerbach. Of course, he was using every possible gimmick to keep the fans stirred up—and the players, if he could.

On a team like the Celtics this becomes difficult. As the years roll on and you play forty-eight minutes of every game, plus all those exhibitions, you develop almost a laissez-faire attitude and it becomes hard work to get yourself psyched up. You have to harass yourself into developing a deep feeling in most cases. Except for the St. Louis of my bitter memories, I probably never get stirred to a fever-pitch. Only occasionally will something come up.

Recognizing this, Auerbach will work hard on the bench to pull something off to get us going. If he can touch the keystone of genuine, legitimate anger over some event, then his team responds.

Mostly, it is a straightforward test of one man's ability against another, rising to a gradual crescendo as we engage in the playoffs. In the playoffs, everyone is stirred.

It was stirring enough that first championship, that's for sure. Midway in the season we had the idea we were going to win it all. We came down the stretch and then beat Syracuse, an old, old rival for the Eastern title and now we went after St. Louis.

They went right back after us.

It was a series with plenty of incidents. Pettit was knocked out. Auerbach came into Kiel Auditorium for the fourth game and Kerner bad-mouthed him about something. Auerbach smacked him in the mouth, knocking him down as Kerner's six strongarm guys gathered around him.

Auerbach came back to the bench fuming, rubbing his

knuckles. "Now you know how I feel in St. Louis, Red," I said.

The seventh and final game was on a Sunday afternoon in Boston Garden. April 13, 1957.

It was fantastic. So they said. I remember very little of it. Just a sea of voices washing over like waves and impressions of arms reaching past and bodies bumping.

Before the game, Auerbach slowly picked St. Louis apart. "Watch Martin do this. Watch Pettit do that. Remember that Macauley can't do this." It was calm and rational in the dressingroom. No hysterics. No promises. We went out to play for the world championship. "You're playing with mah money," Ramsey said.

Cousy and Sharman went dead. They couldn't buy a point. Ramsey, Heinsohn and Russell had a good game. The tide flowed back and forth and we had to go two overtimes to win it.

At the end, Auerbach was jumping up and down, going mad with joy. We cooled him off by throwing him in the shower. Then I shaved my beard off. We were the world champions.

Now, the idea was to hold it.

Tom Heinsohn was Rookie of the Year. Russell was just another player. They said it was because I came in December. Some guys said I was robbed. Some laughed. I figured Heinsohn was a great player. But I hurt inside.

Later, I wrote an article for *Sports Illustrated* and said some things which were highly controversial. This did not exactly make me everyone's idea of the All-American boy.

I meant what I said.

I will not lie for a simple reason—I think too much of myself. You ask me for my opinion and you will get it. The trouble with asking someone's opinion is that most people who ask your opinion don't really want it. They just want their own opinion confirmed.

I felt it was necessary for me to say what I thought about the United States in a time of turmoil and change. I would add only that I said what I thought at that time. Some of my views have changed since then. That was 1958. This is now. Time runs like the flight of geese to the south. It is here and a thing of beauty and gone and time fled through all these tumultuous years and now my views have altered accordingly because circumstances have changed.

I refused to take any money for the article. I have stressed through this book that I am proud of my profession and that in the ultimate sense I am a professional. But I do not hold with men talking about a gut issue who do it only for money. What I had to say had to be said—in my opinion—but for it you do not take money.

If you have to lie to get along or to get a friend then it is not worth it.

So I said what I thought. About the quota, which did exist at that time. About other things. And I slipped into the error that many people make. Because I was very, very angry I began to put people into groups. I blamed the entire white population for what had happened to the Negro in America.

For being called "black gorilla" in St. Louis. For not being the Rookie of the Year. For everything that had ever happened to me.

I said: "I don't like most white people because they are white. Conversely, I like most Negroes because they are black. Show me the lowest, most downtrodden Negro and I will say to you that man is my brother."

It didn't sit well. Sit well? Boy, they were ready to hang me. But I said it. And I lived with it. I have never gone back on it to this day. I make the point only that I said it out of emotion.

The black-white issue in America is perhaps the fault of a white mass which kept the blacks down. But to segregate oneself, and become totally black, is as wrong as the problem itself and will certainly not work towards the solution.

There can be no neutrals in the battle for human rights. If you are for the status quo, then you are against the rights of man, because you are afraid to rock the boat.

Baby, I rocked the boat. And it was a long year after that. They were waiting for me. There have been backlashes of it ever since.

Some personal points here. I have deep-seated views

130

about the problems of the Negro in America. It is my right, influenced by, but not governed by prejudice.

Do I mind being six feet, ten inches tall? No. I think it's a privilege, not a disadvantage. I'm something of an egotist. About my height. About my color. I am proud.

If I had anything to change it would only be that I would have preferred a rich—no, scratch that—a fabulously rich father.

My goals? Among them is the same one we all have —to be rich. What will I do with it?

I have an idea. I do not make myself out to be the great humanitarian of my generation, but I have ideas.

I feel that I was fortunate. Nothing was ever forced on me. I did everything I did by choice. In the matter of human rights, I spoke early. I became completely disenchanted with the civil rights movement at a later time because I think they wanted to compromise on a status quo.

Logic tells me that you have to compromise, but I can never reconcile myself to the fact that there will be a compromise on civil rights.

At first, there were diverse groups. All fighting. All militant. Now, in a sense, they are consolidated and, as far as I am concerned, ineffective. They have stopped fighting.

Martin Luther King is essentially a man of peace. People think of him as a civil rights leader, but this is only one element into which he has moved. Essentially, he desires peace everywhere. Civil rights is something which brought him into worldwide focus, almost a by-product, as it were, of his life's work for peace.

I feel and have always felt that we cannot accept a status quo. With the mandate given Lyndon Baines Johnson —and eternal cynic that I am, I was stunned and pleased at the great lengths to which the President went to fight for civil rights—we should have moved forward and solved the issue permanently.

Instead, we are treading water. Ten years from now, we will have lost ground and will be forced to fight again and it will be harder, much more difficult, because the old methods will no longer work.

This was the time in our lives when the Negro should

131

have moved to the ultimate solution. The Johnson mandate in the election of 1964 was not an accident. It was caused by pressure from the masses. Now the pressure is slowly being reduced.

Everyone says that the Negro now wants to run the country, but this is not so. But the Negro does have a right to conduct himself exactly as would any other sixth generation American.

I think the civil rights movement should continue to exert a force and keep the pressure on, and believe that every Negro over twenty-one should vote rather than follow the normal tendency of sitting back relaxed and saying: "We've got it made." Further, I think every Negro should get out and participate in the mainstream of American life.

The battle lines are basically economic. Economically, I would like to do something for the American Negro. Employ them, not a giving, but an achieving. A chance to achieve a place.

Over-reaching myself? Perhaps. A theory which I am now moving into the field of practical application.

Fear . . . prejudice . . . bitterness.

It is the reactions to these emotions that make a man.

Everyone is born with a prejudice. Every man is born with a fear.

It comes to us at birth's first breath. It leaves us only when we understand and conquer it.

It comes to you regardless of color. If I see you and you are white, then my first reaction is that you are white. If you see me and I am black, then your first reaction is that I am black.

Only when we conquer this first gap do we reclaim our right as men.

From there we go forward to conquer fear . . . and prejudice . . . and bitterness.

The world is made of heroes and cowards and men who are never noticed. Only history—many generations later—can ever judge who was the hero and who was the coward and who was the man not worthy of notice.

In this time and place, then, I am not qualified to make the judgment. I am qualified only to talk of a world which I have seen, a world where I have walked. I have seen reactions to stress and to situations which have made men—and have made cowards.

I acknowledge every man's right to prejudice. Prejudice is native. The man who is not prejudiced—and I do not equate this with race, but with taste, food, air, clothes, books, all the gamut of civilized life—is a liar.

It is in conquering prejudice, however, that he becomes a man.

Did I conquer it? I like to think so. I am still not sure. I will draw my last breath wondering.

But let them inscribe on my tombstone that I was not just an athlete, or a rich man, or a Negro.

Let it be said simply: "Russell. A man."

As I have written this book more and more thoughts and feelings have flooded back to me and I have seen even my own prejudices and learned something from them.

If I had a wish to make on the basis of this printed word, it is that this book should stand up twenty years from now or a hundred years from now as an honest and accurate statement of what the world was like for one man at one time.

I have seen so much in all walks of life. Bitterness. And it has made me react. If it did not affect me then I would be a fool or a man without the right to say I am a man.

But I had to learn to be objective. Sometimes I was not. I have tried to be, but I have failings. This is the honest story of a man. A man with, I hope, some goodness. A man, also with some failings.

This was part and parcel of the story of the championships which we won.

It happened concurrently.

The next year began with Sam Jones coming on board and coming to live with my wife and me. Now I had a roommate. Now we had a goal—another world championship.

We lost it.

We had it in the palm of our hands and we lost it. In the third game of the world championships against St. Louis—and in St. Louis—I came down for a ball and I twisted my ankle. I was finished. I knew it. I tried to go on it, but there wasn't a chance.

133

The Celtics were far from finished. Cousy, Sharman, Ramsey, Heinsohn carried the load. They carried it right to the sixth game, once again in St. Louis. I had a broken bone, but we put a plaster cast on my ankle and I tried to play. Auerbach didn't force me. He said: "Can you go?" I said: "I'll try."

The try lasted about three minutes. I was going nowhere. I was more of a detriment than a help. He took me out of there. It was the right move. Red said: "There will be other seasons, Russ."

There wasn't any other 1958 season. The guys were great. They carried them right to the last second of the sixth game, but then St. Louis won it. If one more shot had gone in, one more play had worked, we would have had the seventh game back in Boston and very possibly, the world championship.

I was MVP that year. But we didn't win the title.

I was still fighting.

One area of the fighting came in moving to an all-white neighborhood in Reading, Massachusetts. I felt this way—I want the best kind of life, the best kind of schools, the best kind of police protection for my family. In our culture, the best is in the white neighborhoods. You don't find it in the Negro areas because they don't get full support of city government. A cold harsh fact. Like it or not.

I would like to pretend that to further the cause of understanding I moved into Reading. I would like to say that I followed an old precept—I went to the white neighborhood to show the whites that Negroes are people and can be lived with, side by side, and that I went knowing full well the strain which would be placed upon us, but that it was for the good of the overall cause.

I didn't. I went because I wanted better things. If anyone learned anything, then it was just a result of what transpired. I wasn't trying to prove a point.

Indeed, I don't know what was learned exactly. The first year our house (isn't that strange?) was robbed twice.

Cars followed me when I drove through the town square late at night. One night, I just stepped on the gas and went through about 110 miles an hour. The car following finally caught me when I got home. It was the police. "Do you know what speed you were going?" the cop asked. "Yeah," I said. "110 miles an hour. I figured if anyone was going to follow me they might as well get their money's worth."

Over the years, the people of Reading and Bill Russell learned to have a mutual respect for each other on the basis of being just decent, average, everyday people.

In fact, the people of Reading gave me a testimonial in 1962. The high school auditorium was sold out. I can only say that I appreciated it. I appreciated it because we were all meeting on equal ground as equal people.

As I said at the testimonial: "I thought the only people who knew me in this town were the police because I drive so fast."

They are good people. No better, no worse than any other, including, incidentally, the police, with whom I have long since established what I like to think is an active friendship.

All part of learning.

All part of my life, as we approached the long sweep of world championships.

For now, we were really going. We had the horses. We were moving. It transfers into one long kaleidoscope of action. Of plane rides and near crashes—which is how I have developed almost a fatalistic belief that having flown over a million miles someday the law of averages will catch up with me.

Of overnight flights which kept us bouncing from town to town. Of clashes, man to man, and games and the eternal, lonely hotel rooms. Tom Heinsohn called the playoffs "the rubber room days." It was his belief that this was the time of the year when everyone would like to be locked in a rubber room with a rubber bat in complete darkness and just whack away at anyone who came along.

Perhaps that was the way my whole life was. The torment of loneliness seemed to weigh heavily on me. What do you do really? Where can you go? Do you drink?

Do you run, run, run, seeking the action, seeking the laughter, seeking forgetfulness?

I don't drink. I figured it was a loser's game. I rolled around, trying to find myself.

Gradually it came. As the years went on, it came more and more and it was really the same thing that had come to me when I was a kid in Oakland. I woke up one day and I had gone to bed just a sixteen-year-old boy and in the morning I was a sixteen-year-old who was proud to be a Negro boy.

Now I was proud to be a Negro man.

The pressures continued, the games had to be played. The opponents had to be faced. There were the slaps in the face from awards which went to Chamberlain, when I felt in my heart that I was best. In five All Star games he was first string. I was second.

But I was the world champion.

And always the games. The games. The games. The games. Riding all night in airplanes. Playing cards, just to pass the time. Playing gags on guys, just to pass the time.

The long summers. Investments in Africa, trips, turmoil.

An occasional brawl. Always the pride of being world champion. They tried. But no one could take it from us.

Yet, through it all, I was confronted with the never-ending search that all Negro males go through for their manhood.

It is a thing you want to scream: "I MUST HAVE MY MANHOOD."

As in 1962, when I took my children south to visit my grandfather, an aged, wonderful man, whose triumphs and frustrations and wisdom have touched the heartbeat of my life and thought.

I love my grandfather, perhaps more than any man in the world, with a kinship which is more than blood and with a laughter that is more than joy. He was and he is a man for all seasons, a great man, and I took my children—one of whom I named for him, Jacob—with me and I went south to my native state.

I was a world champion. I was a man. Yet, from

Washington, D.C. to Louisiana, my children could not stop to eat. My children could not stop to sleep. They rode in the back seat of the car driven by their father, who was their father and a man and a world champion and we could not stop because we were black.

Were I the lowest white trash in the world, I would have been able to stop. But I was black. And I had to keep going. My children had to keep going with the wonder in their eyes that things could change, with the not understanding pleas from the back seat: "Daddy, can't we stop? Daddy, I'm hungry."

All success in the world is relative.

AM I A FOREIGNER IN MY HOMELAND?

Thus does the anger descend upon a man. Thus does it well up and declare the battleground. A field without banners, a fight without bugles. A deadly, personal conflict, where only a man who is a man can survive.

I have survived.

This book is not written in anger. Nor does it seek to expunge the bitter hurts of my lifetime or the lifetime of any man.

Example, only, is what I seek.

Show me a man, any man, he is my brother.

Show me a bigot, any bigot, he is my enemy.

Look, now just to the moment. Perhaps, understand. From the world championship to the children crying in the back seat.

It is part of my story, a story which has value only if people learn and remember. Not for me. Not for the man with the beard. Rather, for the children who cry.

The championships came in one long succession. . . Syracuse . . . Philadelphia . . . St. Louis . . . Los Angeles . . . San Francisco . . . Minneapolis . . . Cincinnati.

Forget it baby. We were going nowhere but up.

But Russell was going nowhere but down.

For years I had been bothered by arthritis of the knees.

I refused to take shots for it. I always refused to take any kind of shot. That is how you really get hurt, reducing pain, but increasing injury and increasing the real

137

pains which will only come years later when unhealed tissue cannot adjust to advancing age

There is a tendency in modern athletics to give shots to dull pain. Don't let them do it to you. Many a kid has been ruined for life trying to be the hero for one moment, which on the basis of a lifetime, becomes insignificant.

The pain never really died and there were games when it was agony. There were plane trips when it was torture not to be able to stretch my legs.

There were the fears which had grown inside me. The plane that was going to crash, a feeling which wasn't helped by some of the rides we had.

In 1963, I rode the slide downhill. I was on the verge of a nervous breakdown. I was crawling the walls and I was unable to control myself.

I very nearly gave it all up. There comes a tide in the life of men . . . but it had not yet come for me. Only a coward quits. Maybe I'm a coward, but I wouldn't.

1963 . . . a vintage year.

This was the year that everyone decided Los Angeles would beat us for the championship. We were finished. Even Los Angeles believed it. They had Baylor and West and one of their few weaknesses was at center where the late Jim Krebs was working alternately with Gene Wiley and Leroy Ellis.

They had style and ability and we were getting older.

The All Star game was at Los Angeles that year and the California radio stations blared all through it: "Los Angeles . . . the basketball capital of the world."

It bothered us. A team can be psyched by a coach but Auerbach couldn't do much to psych us until that routine. L.A. was a challenge and we would have to face it. But never mind the boy scout stuff.

Red also used it to good effect to get the fans steamed up. He rubbed it in everywhere.

We rubbed it in on the court.

To get to L.A. we were going to have to go through the Syracuse Nats. We thought. But Cincinnati pulled off a stunning upset in the Easterns.

We couldn't get excited about it. Cincinnati? Ought to beat them four straight. As a result we got overconfident. They carried us the seven full games. We had half a mind on L.A. instead of on the meat and potatoes.

That's one of the big problems. You get overconfident. They taught us a lesson. Seven games. We were ready for L.A.

It was Cousy's last series.

And all that fru-fraw about the basketball capital of the world. Everyone came to see us get killed. By the time the sixth game arrived the idea passed along that maybe we weren't going to be the lambs led to the slaughter.

We were moving, fast, loose as ashes, and we were shaking L.A. and turning them every way but loose, baby. We had their number.

In the sixth game we needed to win to clinch the title. The Sports Arena was mobbed with people. About 15,000 of them—a full house. National television.

We went out in front and we held it pretty good, then the Lakers started to make a rush at us. Baylor, playing with a bad knee, and West were the two who were killing us.

Baylor is power personified. He just sweats power. He has the touch with his shot and he has a great second effort. He does everything right-handed, though. That was the one edge we had against him.

West is a digger. He is fierce. He hustles. He is a great clutch player and seldom misses down the stretch. He works hard at it because he wants to be great. When he plays defense he can be very good at it.

And they wanted the title. We went to the front in the third quarter and we made the same mistake we always made up until 1964. The Celtics were a defensive team which was offensively minded and at times we would try to sit on a lead. This time we tried to sit on it and Baylor and West brought L.A. back into the game. Rudy LaRusso gave Heinsohn a hard time at one corner to back them up and Dick Barnett kept coming through with that great shot of his.

Up by fourteen, however, it didn't seem that we could lose.

Then, suddenly, Cousy came downcourt, all alone, and spun to the floor with a twisted ankle.

Almost as one person, 15,000 people were on their feet cheering. They figured their team was going to make a run for it with Cooz out of there.

I remember saying to him at the time: "They're giving you the big goodbye because they figure they've got it won."

Cooz just growled. This wasn't the way he wanted to go out, crippled . . . on the bench . . . just watching.

Down the stretch of the next few minutes the Lakers controlled the ball and kept coming closer and with four minutes left to go they tied it up.

Auerbach was jumping up and down. He was fit to be tied. At times like this in the huddles he'll say something, picking apart a player who is going badly.

There was more profanity in that huddle than there ever had been before. Cousy was coming back in and he was swearing like I never heard him before.

I just went over and sat down on the bench. No one has ever known this, but I played that last game with a completely numb pair of legs. It was diagnosed as "complete fatigue." I don't know what it was. Except that I couldn't feel anything from the hips down after the first five minutes. I refused to say anything about it in the press after the game not because I am a great-hearted sportsman, but simply because it was Cousy's game, Cousy's last, fantastic farewell to the sport he graced for so long and it would have been wrong to take even one moment of his greatness from him.

So they stood there in that little circle swearing and I sat on the bench and LeRoux came over and said: "How do they feel?"

"Oh, other than being completely numb, they're great," I answered. "I mean, how many twenty-nine-year-old guys do you know with two-hundred-year-old legs? I feel like I've been embalmed."

LeRoux went back to the circle. I sat there looking out at the people of California. There was a pretty girl in the first row opposite. She was all excited and her legs were crossed. I thought: "I wish my legs felt as good as hers look."

They called time and I stood up.

We were ahead again by two points and it was Los

Angeles' ball. Now came what I believed to be the key play. Baylor was bringing the ball down. A three-pointer gave them the lead. They would hold it once they got hold of it.

This is where the game becomes its best . . . it's greatest personal challenge. This is where frozen thinking, canned thinking, applied psychology comes in.

The mob was yelling. The noise swept over and out of the corner of my eye. I watched Doris Day drop her popcorn in her lap as she jumped with excitement and thought "Not this year, Doris, baby, not this year." I smiled and looked back to Baylor and he was picking up steam and coming down to meet me.

Under pressure, a great player will always go to his best shot. Baylor's best shot was to drive, sink the ball and pick up a charging foul for the extra point.

I would come to his front and he would go around me. But Elgin's best shot also meant that he had to go to his right. He never goes to his left.

I had him dead. He was coming down on me, faking, bobbing, but I knew what his play would be. He would go to his greatness. I went to his front so it would appear he could go around and then took a step and a half to the left at the same moment he cut.

He banged right into me.

And now the long eternity of waiting began. Powers was blowing his whistle. I had tricked Baylor into a charge. But what if Powers called it the other way? Baylor shot the ball as he banged into me. It had gone through the hoop. A foul call against us makes it a three-pointer for him and they win.

Seconds . . . hours . . . years . . . and now Powers made the sign:

Charging.

No basket.

Our ball.

Our world championship.

Cousy was turning now, throwing the ball to the rafters in one last, violent exuberance of victory. The bench was emptying. They were swarming out at us. Ramsey was limping over, waving his arms.

I remember thinking I had to get the ball for Cousy.

141

It was his last game. The ball was coming down and I jumped through some people and grabbed it. Then we were all dancing around, hugging each other and I had an arm around Cousy and an arm around Ramsey and we were going off.

The Los Angeles sports center was suddenly empty. It was the eeriest thing I had ever seen in all my life. Two minutes earlier it had been full of 15,000 people screaming for our blood and now there was only silence and emptiness.

We were alone with our championship.

An hour later we were on a 707 headed for home. I had a magnum of champagne to celebrate, my one annual drink. As I stood in the doorway, I couldn't resist it. I raised the magnum and bowed and said: "As the sun sinks slowly in the west we bid farewell to Los Angeles . . . the basketball capital of the world."

We exited laughing.

Beginning in 1964 everyone figured there was no point in any more laughter. Cousy gone, the story line was that we wouldn't even win the Eastern Championships. Cincinnati was the choice to beat us. "What are you going to do without Cousy?" everyone asked.

We were going to play the game, baby. What did you think we were going to do?

We made one big, but very subtle change. Recognizing that we were now without a key offensive man, Auerbach adjusted us to become the best defensive team in the history of basketball. K.C. Jones and Sam Jones made the backcourt. Sam was the shooter. K.C. was the defensive man.

We picked up Willie Naulls. Heinsohn was one cornerman and Tom Sanders was already developing into the best defensive forward in the game.

Auerbach had always stressed conditioning. That was a secret of the Celtics. We would come out of the box roaring and be so far ahead of other teams after twenty games that they couldn't easily catch up and then we would have them psyched.

This was part of Auerbach's philosophy. Some teams let super stars play themselves into shape, on the theory of the long long season.

Not Auerbach. With him everyone is equal. The only prima donna on the team is Auerbach. Everybody better be in shape.

We were. We came out flying high and won the first fourteen games. Cincinnati? Are you kidding me, baby. We all liked Cousy, but now we had something to prove; we were all world champions, not just playing with one.

We were successful in proving our point. Another season disappeared behind us and in the wake of it wallowed Cincinnati and Wilt Chamberlain's San Francisco.

Another year gone. Another memory. The flash of a remark, of a scene of a place.

Being 6-10, you draw a lot of comments. Especially, if you are a 6-10 Negro with a beard.

Like, when we were coming out for the finals with L.A. in 1963. It turned out to be our final game (as we hoped it would be). The Sheraton-West was full, since the baseball season had started and the Braves were in town for a series with the Dodgers.

So, we were staying at a motel. The motel-owner wanted to treat us right and sent out some station-wagons for us. I was sloping through the airport when this man came up to me and said: "I have a station-wagon outside for you."

I said: "For me? Are you sure you have the right person?"

You should have seen that poor guy. He didn't know what to say. I mean, how many 6-10 Negroes with beards were walking through the airport from the Boston plane?

Just one of the quirks you pick up.

Or the people that ask you: "How's the weather up there?"

Them I walk right by.

Or: "Are you a basketball player?"

To them I say: "No. I'm a jockey."

You learn to shy away from people. Some mean well. Some don't. It's like the haves and the have-nots. The don't people are the ones who bug you. I learned over a long period to watch out for them. As a result, you shy away from everyone.

I broke the code one night in Cincinnati during the

1963 Easterns. A friend of mine went out with me to a place which had a jazz combo. It was midnight and we couldn't sleep. We were sitting in the back of the lounge drinking Seven-ups.

A lady about forty-five came over and asked if I was Bill Russell. I started to say, "No."

But she was a nice little middle-aged matron, so I said: "Yes. I am."

Immediately, she had to sit at my table. Now my friend and I were talking about something that was highly personal. This was an intrusion. But it was late and she was a lady, so we let her sit and then the next thing you know her husband was called over by her and we had a party of four.

Now everybody had to talk and we couldn't hear the music that we came for or discuss what we were concerned with.

But, what the heck, she was down from some town out in the sticks and it was their night to howl, so we were polite. It went on for about twenty minutes. And we were extra polite because she was a lady.

Then she turned to my friend, who was white, and said: "And what do you do? Are you this animal's keeper?"

The cold ice of irritation and anger came pouring forth. I didn't say a word. My friend didn't know what to say. I knew he wanted to stand up and say, "Lady, you and your silly husband scram, you're interfering with our table, our privacy, our world and you weren't invited and now you're insulting."

It was the first time he'd run into it.

Instead he said: "No. He's my keeper. Because I'm the animal."

We paid our bill and we left. What the hell. They never even knew what they did wrong and I never bothered to tell them. In fact, we left very politely and the lady was inviting us to stop and see them if we ever came through Washington Court House, Ohio.

I will endeavor to avoid ever being trapped there.

But it comes up all the time and it slaps you in the face. You have to learn to overcome it and take it in the sense that it is meant. People, sometimes, are just dumb, stupid people. Everybody isn't. Just some.

Ramsey and I were named co-captains the year following Cousy's retirement. I turned the job down, saying: "Hell, Red. You never had co-captains before. One or the other, I don't care. Not two."

In the Auerbach form of democracy we had two. It works. One or the other of us was always on the floor and Ramsey was a good captain. For myself, Auerbach said that I was learning to take hold and be the captain, but I had news for him. I wasn't changing at all. Maybe he was just coming to have another understanding of me.

1963-64 was a horrible personal year. I felt the world coming to an end for me. I was on the verge of a nervous breakdown. I could feel everything slipping away from me.

I had to get away, but I was trapped in a world from which there was no escape. No way out. The knees hurt. The planes always lay one day ahead of us.

It was the long, long season.

There was only one thing to do. Try to find some humor. Try to find some safety valve. Try to fight it and beat it.

How I did it I don't know. But gradually, it ebbed. I woke one morning and the playoffs were beginning and, suddenly, it was all right again and I was whole again. I was Bill Russell again.

I knew at last who I was. And yet I still asked— Who am I, really?

What else can I tell you?

About the long sequence of championships? You'd be bored. Professional sports ultimately becomes just one long, mixed-up scenario of airplanes and practice gyms and games. Game after game after game until you don't remember who you are or where you are. You just look at the schedule and somebody says: "American Airlines, 7:30."

At 7:30 on a dark morning you are at the airport and the plane takes you to the next place and you grab a cab and go to the coffee-shop and have lunch and then kibitz around the hotel all afternoon. You go to a movie or go for a walk and then you eat and then at 6 P.M. you get together in the lobby and take a cab to the sports arena. Your suitcase becomes an extension of your right arm. Always packed, always ready.

You get to the arena and you are ninety minutes from the game and you wait your turn to get taped and try and think of other thoughts and want to just run away, and people come in and shake your hand and say hello and you're polite and then a half hour before the game starts you sit there on the funeral-parlor chair and Auerbach says something to the team.

He seldom gets mad. Once in a while, but not often. He just talks about the opponent and the weaknesses of the opponent. Then someone knocks on the door and yells: "Time."

So you get up and you walk out there and 13,909 people begin yelling: "Russell . . . you're nothing . . . Hey, Bill . . . how's the weather up there? . . . Hey, Russ, I'm with you . . . Hey, Russell, you stink."

You don't even listen. You go through the warm-up motions and then sit down for a minute on the bench and gradually the team comes back to the bench and gathers around and the announcer calls off the starters and you go out to the foul line and stand there and then they play the Star Spangled Banner and you go back to the bench and take your jacket off. Auerbach says something like: "Okay. Go get them." We touch hands in a semicircle and go out and I shake hands with the center for the other team and maybe say a few words, like "How's the family? How's business?" or "Good luck" . . . thinking to myself "You're going to need it."

The ball goes up and from there on it is forty-eight minutes of ferocity and psychology. You think and plan and move according to the best way you know, and you catch the eyes of your teammates and throw them the ball and shove and hook and bull your way to the rebounds and somewhere in the background hear the sea of voices washing over you, condemning you, yelling at you, cheering you.

You try to bring a kid along by giving him confidence and throwing the ball more to him. You try to shock a veteran pro who is afraid to take the ball in a tight game by throwing it right at him. You try to figure a new switch, a play, a pick. You run down and stand and

146

set the pick for your man and let someone bang into you because they can't go around you and, suddenly, it is half-time, and you go back into the locker-room.

On the way in, sometimes, people call you "Bum." Or people say, "Nice going, Bill."

You keep your head down and run in, because this is the rule, always keep moving. Never notice. No one is supposed to stop. If you stop, there can be the pandemonium of a crowd cheering you in victory or a riot because some bum is mad.

In the locker-room, Auerbach doesn't say much if you are winning. He just advises to watch so and so and calls men on key plays or styles.

If you are losing, occasionally he will start yelling: "I mean, what is this thing? A prom or something? You all want to be dancers? I mean, don't you know this is basketball? The heck with it. Let's go home now. I don't want to watch you guys play basketball. You make me throw up."

Auerbach is a clever man. He uses invective only when it really matters. Usually it doesn't. Calm. Restraint. Just point out the facts. Emotion doesn't enter into it usually. When it does, he has the emotion to get us stirred, even if only slightly.

Even throwing things. He did that once and it made an impression. I doubt he'll do it again.

Whatever it is, he gives us the spur.

We go out for the second half and we start again and it is again a sea of faces, a sea of arms and legs and balls being thrown and trying to outthink the other guy.

Down the stretch the score is close and in the time-outs, Auerbach is saying things in the huddle. "Now, K.C. Move in on that man a little more. Don't let him get the ball. Keep him out of it. Havlicek. You're behind the man. Take him in there. Go through. Break his stride. Heinsohn. Will you please stop shooting the ball and pass?"

We go out again and the fast break starts working and suddenly you realize like you would swimming that you are cresting the wave and that it is all downhill.

You have been playing for forty-seven straight minutes, running up and down, now on the fast break you slow down slightly to catch a breath and to be ready on defense, only going to about halfcourt in a slow run and even if you are ahead and have it won and even in Boston some bum will always yell: "Russell . . . hustle . . . for cripes' sake, hustle."

You just keep playing.

Suddenly it is over.

You join the long string of players running back into the runway and down the tunnel to the dressing room and you sit and rest a minute and maybe drink an orange juice and then you are in the shower, laughing if you won, and dressing and LeRoux is saying: "7:30 in the lobby. I'll have the cabs ready."

It is late now and most of the people are gone. The ones that remain ask for an autograph and then you take the back door out of the place and a cab is waiting and as soon as four players are in it you are taken back down to the hotel.

You go to your room and put the suitcase with your uniform in it down and sit there for a while and stare at the walls.

They close in.

You want to yell or scream or bang them. But instead you go down to the coffee-shop and have something to eat. Some of the other players are there and you kibitz awhile. Now, maybe, you go off to some place to relax with them, or maybe you go by yourself, but mostly you go back up to the room and sit there with the square eyes watching the Late, Late Show, being lonely.

And late, late at night, the cheers long since dissipated, you lie down for awhile and stare at the ceiling and then it is 7 A.M. and the phone rings and you get dressed and go to the lobby and when four guys are ready they take a cab and then the next four and you walk through the familiar airport and have a cup of coffee and a doughnut and get in the plane and the seats are too small and your legs hurt and the arthritis in them makes you want to scream and cut them off.

The plane flies along in the morning sun and the gin rummy games start and you pass the cards back and forth or try to sleep and someone says: "Hey, where are we going?"

The answer could be "Los Angeles . . . Philadelphia . . . St. Louis . . . Baltimore . . . Detroit . . . Cincinnati . . . San Francisco."

It doesn't really matter.

The answer really is—another town, another place, another lonely night.

Seven lonely months. The days, the games go on. The cheering fades into the night and you sit there with the walls closing in on you, looking at the marks on the wallpaper by the TV where someone in a moment of anger threw a drink.

There is a dent there and a brown liquid stain where the liquor came down the side of the wall.

A passing monument to a moment of anger.

And you wonder if you aren't the same.

# CHAPTER IX

## FELTON X

When you become a so-called "name" athlete, you get involved in many State Department trips overseas.

Mine started before the Olympics when we went to South America. After the 1959 season, I went to Africa alone.

My first stop was Tripoli where a large press conference had been arranged. I was warned to be careful. Communist writers were present. They would try to embarrass the United States.

The first question was: "Why are you really here?"

I said: "I am here to play basketball and to show the people of Tripoli something about a sport which I love because I believe they will love it, too."

The Communist writer now threw his bomb and I saw our State people flinch: "What's the name of the King?"

What do you do now, baby?

No one had thought to brief me on the political aspects of Tripoli and I didn't have the vaguest idea of the name of the King, or even if there was one.

I figured truth was a better answer than a stutter, so I said:

"I don't know the name of the King. I am not a politician. I am not interested in politics. I'm interested only in teaching basketball. Were I a spy then I would be very well-informed. I have come here only to work with kids."

Suddenly all the press corps were on their feet and giving me a cheer and they were even throwing a few barbed chuckles at the Communist. No one bothered me any more in press conferences.

From Tripoli, I flew to Ethiopia.

The State Department has been labelled "Ugly" in some countries. In Ethiopia, they did not make a strong impression on me.

I was met at the airport by the cultural attaché. I knew he was there by the yell:

"Hey, Bill . . . Hey, Bill . . . Hey, Boy . . ."

Along came this charging American. "You're a big boy, aren't you? Yeh, Bill Boy, you're a big one."

How to make friends.

No Negro man likes to be called "Boy."

We are men . . . not boys. Not some dumb backwoods slave . . . the connotation of "boy" to the Negro is of servitude . . . of being less than a man.

Then he told me: "You'd better apply for your exit visa two weeks in advance. Their system is so bad it will take that long."

Later, when the time came, I got my exit visa in five minutes.

Then they pulled the really classic boner. In the province of Harra, old tribalism is still very much existent. There were two schools and they were separate entities. One tribe, one school, would not talk to the other.

So, the State Department invited them both to a clinic I was conducting.

Talk about a rumble. You should have been there. Stones. Clubs. Fists.

Where was Russell? Where do you think. I was running as fast as anyone else. The only guy who passed me was the charging American from State. Cultural advisor.

There was one memorable experience. I was giving a clinic one day when an escorted limousine drove up. In it was the Lion himself, Haile Selassie. I was invited to join him in the back seat of the car.

The tiny little giant of a man apologized to me for requiring the conference in the automobile, but explained that it simply would not do to have the Emperor looking up at someone 6-10.

Giant? I felt like a pygmy beside him.

We talked on and on for about ten minutes. He spoke impeccable English. Our State people had told me he did not understand the language. Years later, I watched him being interviewed on television. All the questions went through an interpreter and it was explained that he did not speak English.

Yeah.

It was on this first trip to Africa that I was confronted with the deep emotional feeling of returning to a homeland. I was overwhelmed with the beauty and the depth of the land.

I finally found the most beautiful of all in Liberia.

It crystallized in a schoolroom far upcountry. A question and answer period was held and a child asked me: "Why are you here?"

Without even thinking, I answered: "I came here because I believe that somewhere in Africa is my ancestral home. I came here because I am drawn here, like any man, drawn to seek the land of my ancestors."

The kids stood up and cheered. The demonstration touched me so deeply I began to cry and was unable to continue. In that one short statement I had expressed, poured forth a deep, inner feeling I had never previously recognized.

It welled up from deep inside me like something clean and beautiful and new and it is a feeling I have had ever since. America is my native land. To it I owe my fidelity, my trust, my loyalty. Yet, like any man, I am moved to great emotion by the memory of my ancestors and of their triumphs and their despairs.

Perhaps that was one major reason why I invested in Liberia. Mr. Buchanan, the Commissioner of the Department of Public Works, took me on a tour of the countryside and showed me the excellent economic opportunities in Liberia. Indeed, many U.S. firms have deep investments. Later I found some acreage and I thought, "This is it. This is the place." I obtained it. We started with investments in rubber. Since then the plantation has grown considerably and after six years of worrying and pouring in money and frustrations, and learning about business and rubber, we now appear to be on the verge of making a success of it.

152

Believe me, however. It wasn't a present. And it didn't come easy.

Things didn't come easy when I returned to the United States either. There was speculation about my investments in Liberia and my statements about my ancestral home. Was I planning to reject the United States and live in Liberia? Being the usual grouchy guy I can be when pestered with questions which are patently ridiculous —and being deeply frustrated by the continuing unequal (at that time, 1959) struggle for equality—I answered: "Yeah. Maybe I will. I'll get away from you, anyway."

The reporter left out the last sentence. The story just read that I was planning to move to Liberia.

No one could understand that a man can be caught between two worlds. West Africa is my ancestral home. The United States is my native land.

But because of what I said, the avalanche began. From there, it went on and at one point I was being labeled a Black Muslim.

"Felton X" they called me.

For the record—I am not a Black Muslim.

For the record, I am a proud, reasonably happy man, who was blessed by God in being born a Negro. I am happy to be a Negro. I am happy to share in the problems of the Negro here in America. I hope to do more about it. I understand that the Irish are proud of Ireland, the Italians are proud of Italy and the Jews are proud of Israel. Just like them, I am proud of my ancestral home—West Africa.

And as far as being a Black Muslim goes, let me phrase it this way:

Someone asked me if I was in favor of Muslimism. I answered: "I don't know, because I don't know enough about it."

They wrote: Felton X.

A man should not be against something until he has studied it. I was not against Communism until I thoroughly studied it and recognized that the whole theory was not for me.

I am not a Muslim because I cannot intellectually follow their line of reasoning, although I agree with some of the points they make and honor their right to their philosophy.

But a man cannot be against a name. He cannot just be "anti-Muslim." Or "anti-Communist." He must be against the philosophy, having understood it.

Because I am what I am, it was easy for some persons to fail to accept the true answer and instead dismiss it with: "He's a Muslim."

That is their prerogative but, in turn, any thoughtful person must agree that the basic problems of our society which have created an organization such as Muslimism cannot be answered if people react with "He's a Muslim" when confronted with the naked facts of the human rights issue here in the United States.

And if people don't really realize what Black Muslimism was caused by.

If nothing else, it served a unique purpose. It was so far out—so desperately far out—that it caused more people to move towards the center, to move towards a rational way of thought about civil rights.

Yet, for some, Black Muslimism was an answer. It served as a focal point for the torments of men who needed a far out proposal to shock them from their depravity. Men who were dope addicts, drunks, wife beaters, jailbirds, who had fought all their lives against a society they could not comprehend in a manner they could not comprehend, were attracted to Black Muslimism and embraced it.

They didn't realize it, but they were seeking their manhood . . . the manhood so many Negroes have been deprived of.

But for the record . . . Bill Russell already had his manhood. The name is Felton, yes.

But not Felton X.

## CHAPTER X

# HUMAN RIGHTS

And so, the championships came and went, the tumult and the shouting died. Still, for me the fight went on. This is a chapter for the bigoted to pass.

It does not concern basketball. But it is one that had to be written. Without anger. Without bitterness. Because it is part of the book. Part of the man.

The man has lived a life full of sound and fury . . . and loneliness and fear.

The man has told you a story of an American.

An American Negro.

An American Negro basketball player.

If you have read this just as a sports book, then I hope you found much of interest.

If you have read it as a sociological study, then there was much about the problems which I have encountered as a Negro.

If you have read it as the story of a so-called super star and the pressures which society places upon men whom they judge super—they judge, I do not—then you have found it.

If you have read all the passages woven together, then my aims have been fulfilled and you have a broader perspective of a segment of a life in the world at this time.

Long after my basketball world ends, my fight will go on. It is the fight of any American.

For one of the most enjoyable, but frustrating, experiences in the history of man is to be an American Negro at this time. It is the first time in four centuries that the

American Negro can create his own history. To be part of this is one of the most significant things that can happen.

The concept of the United States is probably the most beautiful one ever conceived by man. A land where men can live, die, succeed, or fail on their chosen battlefield. A land where a man—without regard to anything but his personal merits—can attain anything he desires.

A land where success is relative. Because my father is a foundry worker and your father is a doctor does not mean that one is a failure and one is a success as long as they both contribute.

This is a land where man's contribution is made through choice. It is a society that works for man, not that a man works for. This is as it should be. Society is the creation of man. Man should not live for it.

I do not owe a thing to society. I do for it what I wish because if I am motivated to do things which are good for society it is because I want to . . . not because I owe it.

I have been to many places, but I have not been anywhere which was as beautiful as the North American continent . . . from the rolling hills of Vermont which are so sparklingly magnificent in the days of autumn . . . to Carmel by the sea in the warm sunshine of a California spring.

The cities are so large, so busy. The small towns are so quaint. There is so much to see and do that you can never see it all.

It is so, so pretty.

A beautiful world, this country of ours. But, it will never reach its full potential until we exploit and accept the contributions of every man, large or small.

We do not yet accept the American Negro.

Yet, this issue of human rights is the greatest problem ever faced by a nation. It is an American problem and it must be faced by Americans. And solved by Americans.

I believe one of the problems is misinformation . . . misunderstanding. Americans, oddly enough, are generally uninformed about each other. In the growth of our nation, the trite clichés have developed:

All Italians love lasagne.

The Irish drink.

Every Jew is rich.

The result is misunderstanding. Children hear these stories and develop along these guidelines. Only when they break through barriers and come to understand on a person-to-person relationship are the false tales put to death.

One of the great problems of the black and white struggle is that there has never been a people-to-people relationship.

Most white Americans feel superior to black Americans. This is understandable simply because of a situation which is as old as the history of our land. The Negro has been a slave for four centuries and since Emancipation has been at the bottom of the social strata.

So naturally, even the poorest white says: "Well, I'm not at the bottom. So I'm better."

Very few ask: "Am I better? Am I really better?"

I ask: "Does not slavery affect the slaveholder as well as the slave?"

This issue has many facets.

To me, it is a fact that our success in the United States is judged almost entirely on the gold standard. Thus the most important area of attack must be economics.

Employers say: "I want to hire a Negro, I can't find a qualified applicant."

Why can't they find them?

First, for many, many years, the trade unions would not give a Negro an apprenticeship. A big void was created. All of a sudden, employers want Negro technicians. But, like most Americans, Negroes are practical. If a Negro studied to be a biochemist and became a pullman porter because he could not get any other job, then he is not going to encourage his son to study biochemistry.

A boy dreams that he will be a pilot. Yet, if he is Negro, he will not become one. There are few commercial pilots in the United States who are Negro. Thus, when the airlines call for them, there is still a void. They can't just be manufactured.

And the power structure says: "See, the Negro just can't do this kind of job."

The effect of all of this on the American Negro was to make him aim lower. Instead of being president of the company, he just wanted to get a good job. He compromised and settled for a job which was second best.

A boy can say of his father: "My dad works at the bank." His father has a prestige job. But it is only that of a clerk. And over the years, despite his qualifications, he remains a clerk.

The American Negro is not lazy, but has become unambitious in a sense from the certain knowledge that a limit must be set on his ambitions.

It would never occur to a Negro boy growing up to dream of one day being President. He would be laughed at. "Hell, son, you can't even be a cop. How can you be President?"

As a child this was a subtle confrontation. The daydreams of a boy were filled with limited horizons. You dream. But you never dream to the top.

I dream to be the foreman of the sawmill down the road. But I settle to be an assistant and when I grow up and achieve my failure, I rationalize it.

Result: stifling of ambition.

Lazy? No. This country was built on the cheap labor of the immigrants and the Negroes and on slave labor. These people are the same blood as those who are building new nations now in Africa.

Lazy? Never.

But with a lack of people-to-people understanding, the world has accepted this as a theory.

So many theories. Negores don't take care of their neighborhoods. People will say: "I lived there and it was a lovely place. And then they moved in."

I ask them: When did you live there? Twenty-five years ago? It's the same house, the same neighborhood, but it is twenty-five years older . . . and twenty-five years without paint, or paper, or maintenance.

Because the Negro is fighting to survive, fighting just to pay the rent, in a ghetto where the landlord is an absentee. The landlord—the slumlord—will not repair the property. He bleeds it. The Negro cannot afford to make major repairs. And should he? Does the white tenant in a better neighborhood paint the outside of his rented apartment, or repair the steps?

They say: "The Negro throws garbage in the street."

They do not know that the city government does not collect the garbage regularly. Nor sweep the streets.

Then the Negro breaks through the economic barrier and moves to suburbia. Immediately, he must prove he is "as good as they are." He is begging, not confronting the world with the fact that he is equal as a man.

The relationship between the white and the Negro is most often represented by the police—the symbol of authority. The police are harassed enough already, but as far as the Negro is concerned, the police have completely flunked in the field of human relations.

Even today, most Negroes look on the police as the white man with a badge, the symbol of the white man's authority. The policeman becomes a natural enemy.

This one thing must be remembered. Just as this man was not born a policeman, neither were the Negroes born disliking and hating him. It is a two-sided devil.

The question—which came first?

Where does it end?

It ends somewhere far ahead of us.

I have said that I have become disenchanted with the civil rights movement. I do not believe there should be more compromises. I know it is not practical, but I still believe there should not be.

Right is right.

I endeavor to talk reasonably and rationally. But this is an emotional issue and when emotion is involved you are talking people.

Civil rights today has become too tranquil, too filled with compromise. A few years back it was superb. One big voice. Two million, three hundred thousand Negroes saying as one: "I am dissatisfied."

But disunity set in from the outset. The march on Washington was brilliantly conceived and badly executed. The bigots will make something of this. But I concur with what Malcolm X said: "They merely marched from the feet of one dead President to the feet of another."

From the Washington Monument to the Lincoln Monument. One big voice which was to say: "We are dissatisfied." One big black march, speaking for the Negroes of America.

I think they were in error right at the outset when the idea was compromised by including whites. I do not mean to fault them—either the average, everyday citizen who marched, or the famous ones who stood in front.

But, you see, this was one time—the first time—when Negroes should have stood together alone—representing all Negroes.

Then, they might have done more with the power bloc. Instead, they began in a situation which led to compromise. And they began feuding among themselves, fighting for power. Any organization such as that can be defeated.

Is defeated.

In this very march which became nothing more than a mere picnic, we would not let some of our own leaders from the battlegrounds of the south speak.

And many of the Negro leaders who had compromised for years and compelled the status quo suddenly found it very fashionable to be speakers.

They were around for a long time. But in the bad days of the struggle, they would say: "Oh, I'm not involved. I'm only a politician . . . or an entertainer . . . or a lawyer . . . or a doctor."

The status seekers.

But not the fighters.

Thus the civil rights movement of today, 1965, has become stagnant. Many tremendous things were done by President Johnson. Great, marvelous, visionary achievements.

But now we all overlook the fact that the responsibility is on us to undo within the next two or three years what it took three centuries to create. We must undo a whole thinking process . . . and we only have these few years to accomplish the goal.

To accomplish such a goal, you must do it from many approaches and here is the major weakness of the movement—they have stagnated and become consolidated. When you can consolidate a group into one single force, then you can locate the enemy and defeat it . . . and there are enemies abroad in this land who seek to defeat it.

The black man and the poor white man are in the same position economically. They are both a source of cheap labor as long as they are at each other's throat. They are so busy fighting each other they do not have a chance to look around and see what is going on and how they are being exploited.

As long as you have isolation unionism—a black union and a white union—they can be played off against each other. The result is a deprived people on both sides. They are the uneducated.

Education is of such importance. These threats to close schools are so stupid—punishing the children of both races.

Yet this lack of education has been permitted—and in a sense condoned—by the church, and I mean all churches, just as slavery was condoned 101 years ago.

If segregation and slavery are wrong now, then they were wrong then. The church did not lead us out of the morass.

I may be wrong, but I have always felt that the church must lead. But, alas, it has followed.

None of the breakthroughs in this struggle were initiated by the church. It was only after little people started it that the forces of the church—all churches, all religions—came to bear.

Being now involved, they must learn to lead, to throw their full force behind the struggle in the next three years.

Throughout the civil rights movement—which I prefer to call the issue of human rights—many have taken public positions. Yet during the riots in Los Angeles in 1965, these same people would not take a stand.

This is an inherent danger. They must take a stand. They must be willing to stand up when things go wrong, and enforce right.

And there must be more understanding of the ones who really fight the battle.

It is nice for a bishop's wife like Mrs. Peabody to go to St. Augustine and be arrested.

But it is the people—the whites and the Negroes—

who *inhabit* the battleground day after day and night after night who are the true warriors. Their voices must be heard. Their judgments must be rendered. Their desires must be heeded. Their counsels must be sought.

Human rights is just as complex as any other political problem. The only element on which we can all agree is that the problem must be solved.

There are many different ways. For every one, there should be a leader.

What do I hope to do?

First, help the Negro regain his manhood.

The Negro man has suffered from his own failures in this country.

Because he has been downtrodden, he has lost belief in himself. He has lost his faith.

He has lost his manhood.

The women lost respect.

Then they in turn lost respect for their men.

In gaining true equality, the Negro man must first fight the long battle to regain his rights as a man, to renew his respect for women . . . and their respect for him.

This can only come from within. It can only be created by giving the Negro man the same rights economically. This is what I will try to do. To create, in whatever small way, an economic world for the Negro which gives him nothing, but provides the opportunity to fight to achieve everything.

For some, politics is the answer. I do not believe I could be a politician for I cannot grasp the art of compromise.

But I believe I can be a businessman. And businessmen form pressure groups. I know from my own experience that the chairman of any large company is on a first name basis with the chairmen of at least twenty-five other firms. When he meets with them, when they plan political support, their words—and the thrust of the economy they control—carry force, carry influence.

Not to control. But to have a say. To communicate. To assist one's people economically and to have a say. To be a voice which speaks for them and a voice which will be heard. This, I believe, though devoid of power and only a voice working for a mass, can result, in the far, far future, in the Utopia which all men regardless of color basically seek.

The fight will be long and hard and it will not be won in my lifetime. But the issue is here. Silence in this matter would only be bigotry and we have enough bigots, black and white.

It would be easy to say "Why blame me?" The Germans said that after Auschwitz. But there would not have been an Auschwitz if a man stood up to fight for what he believed or, even, if a man raised his head to ask the mere basic question of humanity: "Why these people? I cannot believe these people are bad because they are Jewish. I will not countenance their treatment because they are from a ghetto, another religion, another kind of world."

No one asked the question and the Jews died at Auschwitz.

Here, in this land, the question must be asked.

No longer can we merely go along quietly.

When I was in college, we played New Orleans. The Negro players stayed on the campus at Xavier University. The whites lived in a hotel downtown.

The year was 1955. The idea was, go along with it. Show everyone that you were human. We saw our teammates only to practice and to play our winning games. No teammate asked the question. No Negro asked the question. And so, the cold, harsh fact remained.

I made up my mind then that I had been wrong. It is not enough to go along, to try to do the gentlemanly thing. Far better to accept the disputes of the world, the harassments, the arguments, the tensions, the slanders, the violence. Raise the question. Confront the blameless ones. We are all to blame.

We all must be confronted.

Only by this means can the Negro man fully regain his manhood. The Negro has come a far distance in a short period of time. It has been but one century since the Civil War.

It has been a century in which many Negroes have gained prominence and wealth and even have attempted a tacit kind of "passing" by not rocking the boat, by not taking their stand, by not asking the question.

They have not joined. They have compromised. They may have ascended to great heights in business, in politics, in education. Yet, because they would not fight, because they would not ask the question, even to them it happened. Their greatness was nothing, for behind their backs men said:

"Nigger."

Others fought.

No man gains a right to the world who will compromise.

It is not a matter for violence. It is a matter for confrontation. It is a matter of asking the question.

And some day, it will work.

Because men who ask have always succeeded . . . or been followed by men who have succeeded.

# CHAPTER XI

## THE BATTLEGROUND

It was July 1963, and the phone rang at my home in Reading, Massachusetts.

Charlie Evers was on the phone from Jackson, Mississippi.

He said: "When Medgar was shot you told me you'd do anything you could to help. I can use some help right now. But you may get killed."

He wanted me in Mississippi two days later to give basketball clinics. The City of Jackson was torn with violence. Other towns came later. Selma . . . Birmingham . . . Bogalusa . . . Oxford . . . the roll-call of the battles of our generation in the 1960s.

I didn't want to go to Mississippi. I was like anyone else. I was afraid to get killed.

My wife asked me not to go. Some friends said the same thing. A man must do what he thinks is right. I called Eastern Airlines and ordered my ticket.

Thirty-six hours later I was playing for a different kind of championship in Jackson, Mississippi. The baggage agent at Eastern couldn't find my suitcase. "You sure you had one, boy?"

I had one, baby.

I had been forewarned. I knew what I was getting into. Jackson was another skirmish in a long battle. The red-necks were out to fight one more delaying action, one more last stand.

Men like Medgar Evers were dead and other men had taken up his flag. Charlie Evers was a man marked for death, who slept with a pistol in his hand. The first night

165

in Jackson I had no pistol, but I stayed with a friend with the door bolted. It would be rattled once in a while. There were noises in the alley. My friend couldn't sleep. "They're coming for us, they're after us," he said.

The kind of men who come after you in the darkness do not frighten me. I went to sleep.

The next day I started giving my basketball clinics. They were the first integrated clinics ever held in the Jackson Auditorium.

There was no trouble in the Auditorium. The Mayor was even pleased, proud, that Jackson could hold such an event.

I was not proud or pleased. It was a century in coming. I could hold clinics anywhere in the world—except in certain places in the United States.

But I was in Jackson to stay for three days. No one was going to drive me out. And no papers were going to print big stories about Bill Russell. It was just something I had to do. Not for credit. Just because I was a man.

At night, darkness came down on the no-man's land which is the Negro segment of the world south of Washington, D.C. Cars followed us down the road. Full of drunken red-necks. Later, they would shoot a soldier, a lady, a kid. They would shoot the unarmed ones. They would lose their taste for it when they came abreast of our car. They would see guns and they would pull back and fall away, the headlights fading into the background.

A coward will never fight a man who is equal. The sadness is that in the darkness of Jackson it had to be men who were equal only with guns.

I was having dinner in Jackson with two priests. Four red-necks came in. Paunchy, sick, loudmouth men who were drinking. They showed their guns as they took the table next to us. They began talking about the priests. I am not overly religious, but they were good men. I said: "I know how you are at praying, but can you fight?" I laughed. They laughed back. The red-necks kept on our backs.

I stood up and went to their table. My knees were shaking. Was it anger? Was it fear?

I stood beside the big one. "Baby," I said, "I am a peaceful man. But to me life is a jungle. When people threaten me or mine, then I go back to the law of the jungle. Now I tell you—which law are we living by here? Because if this is the jungle then I am going to start killing."

They jumped up and left. The priests and I went back to our supper.

Was it hatred?

Was it bitter anger?

Who am I?

Why should I go through this?

I am, in the final sense, just a man. I am neither all right nor all wrong. I was born in this nation, in this century. I was born to be a member of the nation, a member of the century, a member of the world.

A man, nothing more.

Neither right nor wrong.

Maybe I've soured on life, or maybe I'm a cynic, but I wasn't born that way. Maybe, I am an idealist—a frustrated idealist—but I wasn't born that way either. Things that I have experienced have made me what I am.

All I have finally asked is for everybody to succeed or fail on their own merits. I have tried to have a difference in values as values are computed in our modern society. I have worked hard for money. But I have not worshiped it.

I have never worked to be well-liked or well-loved, but only to be respected. I have fought a problem the only way I know how. Maybe it was right or wrong in the approach, but a man can only ultimately be counted if he thinks he is doing right. Then, at least, he is a man.

In this book, I think that some of the problems of being a man, being a super star, being a Negro in the United States today have been pointed out.

I have my own ideas for the future.

I have my own hopes and my own dreams.

I believe that I can contribute something far more important than mere basketball.

I said before three emotions have always been very real to me—fear, prejudice and bitterness.

It is the reactions to these emotions that make a man.

In the end, I live with the hopes that when I die, it
will be inscribed for me:
Bill Russell.
He was a man.

# EPILOGUE

The years go by. The threat of death—a premonition I have always had that I will die one day in an airplane —hangs over me again as I finish these pages and begin another basketball season.

The greater threat of an unequal society lies before me . . . the ultimate challenge for my generation.

The bitterness has ebbed, only to flow again in the form of questions, of hurts which come like a death stroke in a moment of sudden laughter.

They are the hateful things which leave you wondering. How do you fight? How do you restrain your own prejudices?

Why does it hurt when I am so old now?

Why does it still hurt when I have seen it so much?

It happened to my daughter this summer. She is three years old. I named her Kenyatta because it means "Burning Spear" and because it will always remind her of the beauty of Africa and the beauty of the noble race from which she is descended.

She was walking down the beach one day with a white woman. Three years old and hand-in-hand and laughing as the waves washed at her feet.

And a man came along and said: "Nigger . . . they should send all you black baboons back to Africa."

My daughter smiled at him.

Why do they do it?

Are we not human?

My son, Jacob, was six years old this summer. He was visiting with friends. A kid came into a mixed group of Negroes and whites. The children had all played together for several years and there had never been an incident.

Now, this boy, bigger, about twelve, perhaps just stupid and not even from the immediate neighborhood, said:

"You're a nigger."

"No," my son said. "I'm Jacob."

The big boy went away. He never came back.

But why?

Why my son?

He was only Jacob.

We have lived with it. We will continue. Success in business, success in basketball is only the lesser goal. The future lies in our young. We of the old can now only help to guide the young. Not black . . . not white . . . not yellow. Just, the children.

For all my battles, I have learned just that. We, white and black, on one side or on the other, have made our prejudices and our philosophies and now fight our battles.

Pray God, that in the future our children will not have to.

To them all—the centurions of my life—the athletes, the fans, the allies, the foes, whomever they were; the fighters who fought because they believed, I offer only the final thought:

The children.

It is not *"Vale,* Centurions."

It is . . . it must be . . . *"Vale,* our lovely, lovely children."

"THERE IS NOTHING MORE POWERFUL THAN AN IDEA WHOSE TIME HAS COME"

—*Victor Hugo*

# APPENDIX

## BILL RUSSELL'S

## ALL-TIME ALL-STAR TEAM

Jerry West, Los Angeles—Guard
Oscar Robertson, Cincinnati—Guard
Wilt Chamberlain, Philadelphia—Center
Bob Pettit, St. Louis—Forward
Elgin Baylor, Los Angeles—Forward

I might make a change at center, though, if you'll pardon a personal prejudice.

As an alternate, I'd also have to pick Dolph Schayes of Syracuse in his playing days and as coach of Philadelphia. And, of course, the great Bob Cousy.

Best team? Boston Celtics, 1965. Reason: they played the great defense, the Big D as we called it. In any sport, the best defensive team always has to come out in front. That was why the Celtics won in 1965. The Big D.

# PLAYOFF RECORD

| Sea.—Team | G. | Min. | FGA. | FGM. | Pct. | FTA. | FTM. | Pct. | Reb. | Ast. | PF. | Disq. | Pts. | Avg. |
|---|---|---|---|---|---|---|---|---|---|---|---|---|---|---|
| 56-57—Boston | 10 | 409 | 158 | 54 | .365 | 61 | 31 | .508 | 244 | 32 | 41 | 1 | 139 | 13.9 |
| 57-58—Boston | 9 | 355 | 133 | 48 | .361 | 66 | 40 | .606 | 221 | 24 | 24 | 0 | 136 | 15.1 |
| 58-59—Boston | 11 | 496 | 159 | 65 | .409 | 67 | 41 | .612 | 305 | 40 | 28 | 1 | 171 | 15.5 |
| 59-60—Boston | 13 | 572 | 206 | 94 | .456 | 75 | 53 | .707 | 336 | 38 | 38 | 1 | 241 | 18.5 |
| 60-61—Boston | 10 | 462 | 171 | 73 | .427 | 86 | 45 | .523 | 299 | 48 | 24 | 0 | 191 | 19.1 |
| 61-62—Boston | 14 | 672 | 253 | 116 | .458 | 113 | 82 | .726 | 370 | 70 | 49 | 0 | 314 | 22.4 |
| 62-63—Boston | 13 | 617 | 212 | 96 | .453 | 109 | 72 | .661 | 326 | 66 | 36 | 0 | 264 | 20.3 |
| 63-64—Boston | 10 | 451 | 132 | 47 | .356 | 67 | 37 | .552 | 272 | 44 | 23 | 0 | 131 | 13.1 |
| 64-65—Boston | 12 | 561 | 150 | 79 | .527 | 76 | 40 | .526 | 302 | 76 | 43 | 2 | 198 | 16.5 |
| 65-66—Boston | 17 | 814 | 261 | 124 | .475 | 123 | 76 | .618 | 428 | 85 | 60 | 0 | 324 | 19.1 |
| 66-67—Boston | 9 | 390 | 86 | 31 | .360 | 52 | 33 | .635 | 198 | 50 | 32 | 1 | 95 | 10.6 |
| 67-68—Boston | 19 | 869 | 242 | 99 | .409 | 130 | 76 | .585 | 434 | 99 | 73 | 1 | 274 | 14.4 |
| 68-69—Boston | 18 | 829 | 182 | 77 | .423 | 81 | 41 | .506 | 369 | 98 | 65 | 1 | 195 | 10.8 |
| Totals.... | 165 | 7497 | 2335 | 1003 | .430 | 1106 | 667 | .603 | 4104 | 770 | 536 | 8 | 2673 | 16.2 |

## ALL-STAR GAME RECORD

| Season—Team | Min. | FGA. | FGM. | Pct. | FTA. | FTM. | Pct. | Reb. | Ast. | PF. | Disq. | Pts. |
|---|---|---|---|---|---|---|---|---|---|---|---|---|
| 1958—Boston | 26 | 12 | 5 | .417 | 3 | 1 | .333 | 11 | 2 | 5 | 0 | 11 |
| 1959—Boston | 27 | 10 | 3 | .300 | 1 | 1 | 1.000 | 9 | 1 | 4 | 0 | 7 |
| 1960—Boston | 27 | 7 | 3 | .429 | 2 | 0 | .000 | 8 | 3 | 1 | 0 | 6 |
| 1961—Boston | 28 | 15 | 9 | .600 | 8 | 6 | .750 | 11 | 1 | 2 | 0 | 24 |
| 1962—Boston | 27 | 12 | 5 | .417 | 3 | 2 | .667 | 12 | 2 | 2 | 0 | 12 |
| 1963—Boston | 37 | 14 | 8 | .571 | 4 | 3 | .750 | 24 | 5 | 3 | 0 | 19 |
| 1964—Boston | 42 | 13 | 6 | .462 | 2 | 1 | .500 | 21 | 5 | 4 | 0 | 13 |
| 1965—Boston | 33 | 12 | 7 | .583 | 9 | 3 | .333 | 13 | 5 | 6 | 1 | 17 |
| 1966—Boston | 23 | 6 | 1 | .167 | 0 | 0 | .000 | 10 | 2 | 2 | 0 | 2 |
| 1967—Boston | 22 | 2 | 1 | .500 | 0 | 0 | .000 | 5 | 5 | 2 | 0 | 2 |
| 1968—Boston | 23 | 4 | 2 | .500 | 0 | 0 | .000 | 9 | 8 | 5 | 0 | 4 |
| 1969—Boston | 28 | 4 | 1 | .250 | 2 | 1 | .500 | 6 | 3 | 1 | 0 | 3 |
| Totals... | 343 | 111 | 51 | .459 | 34 | 18 | .529 | 139 | 39 | 37 | 1 | 120 |

# LIFETIME NBA RECORD
## BILL RUSSELL

Born February 12, 1934. Height 6.10. Weight 220.
Alma Mater—San Francisco '56.

| Sea.—Team | G. | Min. | FGA. | FGM. | Pct. | FTA. | FTM. | Pct. | Reb. | Ast. | PF. | Disq. | Pts. | Avg. |
|---|---|---|---|---|---|---|---|---|---|---|---|---|---|---|
| 56-57—Boston | 48 | 1695 | 649 | 277 | .427 | 309 | 152 | .492 | 943 | 88 | 143 | 2 | 706 | 14.7 |
| 57-58—Boston | 69 | 2640 | 1032 | 456 | .442 | 443 | 230 | .519 | 1564 | 202 | 181 | 2 | 1142 | 16.6 |
| 58-59—Boston | 70 | 2979 | 997 | 456 | .457 | 428 | 256 | .598 | 1612 | 222 | 161 | 3 | 1168 | 16.7 |
| 59-60—Boston | 74 | 3146 | 1189 | 555 | .467 | 392 | 240 | .612 | 1778 | 277 | 210 | 0 | 1350 | 18.2 |
| 60-61—Boston | 78 | 3458 | 1250 | 532 | .426 | 469 | 258 | .550 | 1868 | 264 | 164 | 0 | 1322 | 16.9 |
| 61-62—Boston | 76 | 3433 | 1258 | 575 | .457 | 481 | 286 | .594 | 1891 | 341 | 207 | 3 | 1436 | 18.9 |
| 62-63—Boston | 78 | 3500 | 1182 | 511 | .432 | 517 | 287 | .555 | 1843 | 348 | 189 | 1 | 1309 | 16.8 |
| 63-64—Boston | 78 | 3482 | 1077 | 466 | .433 | 429 | 236 | .550 | 1930 | 370 | 190 | 0 | 1168 | 15.0 |
| 64-65—Boston | 78 | 3466 | 980 | 429 | .438 | 426 | 244 | .573 | 1878 | 410 | 204 | 1 | 1102 | 14.1 |
| 65-66—Boston | 78 | 3386 | 943 | 391 | .415 | 405 | 223 | .551 | 1779 | 371 | 221 | 4 | 1005 | 12.9 |
| 66-67—Boston | 81 | 3297 | 870 | 395 | .454 | 467 | 285 | .610 | 1700 | 472 | 258 | 4 | 1075 | 13.4 |
| 67-68—Boston | 78 | 2953 | 858 | 365 | .425 | 460 | 247 | .537 | 1451 | 357 | 242 | 2 | 977 | 12.5 |
| 68-69—Boston | 77 | 3291 | 645 | 279 | .433 | 388 | 204 | .526 | 1484 | 374 | 231 | 2 | 762 | 9.9 |
| Totals . . . | 963 | 40726 | 12930 | 5687 | .440 | 5614 | 3148 | .561 | 21721 | 4096 | 2601 | 24 | 14522 | 15.1 |

# WINNERS OF YEARLY TOP HONORS

| Year | Outstanding Player | Rookie of Year |
|------|-------------------|----------------|
| 1950-51—. . . . . . . . . . . . . . . . . . . . | | . . . . . . . . . . . . . . . . . . . . . . . . . |
| 1951-52—. . . . . . . . . . . . . . . . . . . | | . . . . . . . . . . . . . . . . . . . . . . . . . |
| 1952-53—. . . . . . . . . . . . . . . . . . . | | Don Meineke, Ft. W. |
| 1953-54—. . . . . . . . . . . . . . . . . . . | | Ray Felix, Baltimore |
| 1954-55—. . . . . . . . . . . . . . . . . . . | | Bob Pettit, Milw. |
| 1955-56—Bob Pettit, St. Louis | | Maurice Stokes, Roc. |
| 1956-57—Bob Cousy, Boston | | Tom Heinsohn, Bos. |
| 1957-58—Bill Russell, Boston | | W. Sauldsberry, Phil. |
| 1958-59—Bob Pettit, St. Louis | | Elgin Baylor, Mpls. |
| 1959-60—Wilt Chamberlain, Phil. | | W. Chamberlain, Phil. |
| 1960-61—Bill Russell, Boston | | O. Robertson, Cinn. |
| 1961-62—Bill Russell, Boston | | Walt Bellamy, Chi. |
| 1962-63—Bill Russell, Boston | | T. Dischinger, Chi. |
| 1963-64—Wilt Chamberlain, S. F. | | Jerry Lucas, Cinn. |
| 1964-65—Bill Russell, Boston | | Willis Reed, N. Y. |
| 1965-66—Wilt Chamberlain, Phil. | | Rick Barry, San Francisco |
| 1966-67—Wilt Chamberlain, Phil. | | Dave Bing, Detroit |
| 1967-68—Wilt Chamberlain, Phil. | | Earl Monroe, Baltimore |
| 1968-69—Wes Unseld, Baltimore | | Wes Unseld, Baltimore |
| 1969-70—Willis Reed, New York | | Lew Alcindor, Milwaukee |
| 1970-71—Lew Alcindor, Milwaukee | | Dave Cowens, Boston, and Geoff Petrie, Portland |

## ALL-TIME NBA TEAM

In a poll of the sports editors of the nation's 100 largest newspapers, the Academy of Sports selected the following as the all-time NBA team:

| | | | |
|---|---|---|---|
| 69% | Bob Cousy | 51% | Oscar Robertson |
| 67% | Bill Russell | 49% | Bob Pettit |
| 65% | George Mikan | 33% | Dolph Schayes |
| 57% | Elgin Baylor | 30% | Paul Arizin |
| 53% | Wilt Chamberlain | 15% | Jim Pollard |

## NBA SILVER ANNIVERSARY TOP TEN

| Player | Pos. | Years | G. | FGM | FTM | Reb. | Ast. | Pts. | Avg. |
|---|---|---|---|---|---|---|---|---|---|
| Bob Pettit............ | F | 1954-65 | 792 | 7349 | 6182 | 12851 | 2369 | 20880 | 26.4 |
| Dolph Schayes......... | F | 1948-64 | 1059 | 6135 | 6979 | 11251 | 3071 | 19249 | 18.2 |
| Paul Arizin........... | F | 1950-62 | 713 | 5628 | 5010 | 6129 | 1665 | 16266 | 22.8 |
| Joe Fulks............ | F | 1946-54 | 489 | 2824 | 2355 | 1379 | 587 | 8003 | 16.4 |
| Bill Russell.......... | C | 1956-69 | 963 | 5687 | 3148 | 21721 | 4096 | 14522 | 15.1 |
| George Mikan......... | C | 1946-56 | 520 | 4097 | 3570 | 4167 | 1245 | 11764 | 22.6 |
| Bob Cousy........... | G | 1950-70 | 924 | 6168 | 4624 | 4794 | 6959 | 16960 | 18.4 |
| Bill Sharman......... | G | 1950-61 | 710 | 4761 | 3143 | 2779 | 2111 | 12665 | 17.8 |
| Bob Davies........... | G | 1946-55 | 569 | 2720 | 2331 | 980 | 2050 | 7771 | 13.7 |
| Sam Jones........... | G | 1957-69 | 872 | 6258 | 2864 | 4319 | 2203 | 15380 | 17.6 |